# Contents

# To the student

This book can really help you to increase your English vocabulary while having fun. Most of the tests cover a particular vocabulary area - for example, things in the kitchen, films and TV, IT and computers, business and industry, and so on. Others are based on word types - for example, prepositions, phrasal verbs or collective nouns. There are also tests on rhyming, words, words that sound the same and words that belong in the same group. Just choose the vocabulary area or word type you want to work on, and use the contents list to find the right test for you. Or simply choose a test because you like the look of the activity or the illustration on that page. So if you feel like doing a crossword, choose a crossword. If you feel like looking at cartoons, try one of the tests where you match a caption to a picture. Enjoying the tests is the surest way of learning new words fast. There's no need to start at the beginning and work through every test in the book. The tests at the end are no harder than the ones at the beginning.

There are tip boxes for many of the tests. Some point you to other tests in the same vocabulary area. Others give cultural information related to words on that page. There are also jokes, tips on ways to learn vocabulary, and notes on spelling patterns.

To get new words fixed in your mind, you will need to do each test more than once. So use a pencil to write the answers in the book when you test yourself. Then, when you've checked your answers and looked carefully at the words you didn't know or got wrong, you can rub out your answers ready for the next time you try that test. Each test will take you between five and fifteen minutes to do the first time, but the next time you do it you will probably be much quicker.

There is no progression in difficulty within each book. However, the five books in the Test Your Vocabulary series are carefully graded from Book 1, which is for beginners, to Book 5, which is for advanced students. If you find this book is too hard for you, try the next one down.

Good luck with learning the words in this book. And we hope you enjoy using the words in real situations once you've learnt them here.

Peter Watcyn-Jones and Mark Farrell

# 1 Animals

Write the number of the picture next to the correct word.

badger __4__          hedgehog _____          slug _____

bat _____             mole _____              sparrow _____

deer _____            newt _____              swallow _____

eel _____             otter _____             woodpecker _____

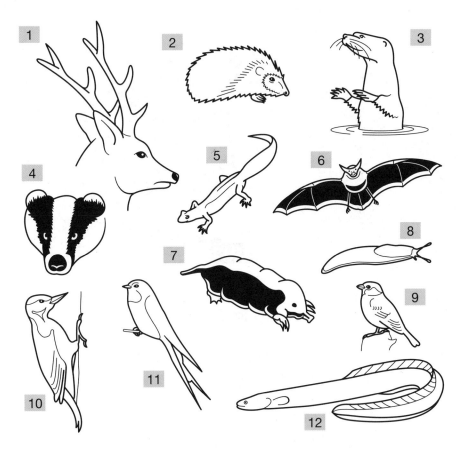

 Quite a few animals keep their singular form for the plural, like *sheep* and *fish*. Most species of fish do the same: *salmon, trout, cod* and so on. Your dictionary should tell you irregular plural forms, so why not check the other animals on this list? Check out Test 35 for more practice with words to do with animals.

# 2 Travelling words

Complete the sentences using words from the box.

> cruise    expedition    ~~flight~~    hike    journey    outing
> package holiday    safari    tour    travel    trip    voyage

1   It was an awful ___*flight*___ – there was lots of turbulence, and one of the cabin attendants actually fell over.

2   The cost of _____ has fallen steadily, which is nice for us but not great for the environment.

3   *From Vienna to Vladivostok* is a book about an amazing train ___journey___ across Russia.

4   Tragically, the *Titanic* sank on her maiden _____ .

5   I met my husband on a romantic ___cruise___ around the Caribbean. He was sea-sick and I nursed him.

6   Do you want to come on a day-_trip_ to Cambridge?

7   The annual school _Paul M_ was always to the same place, Stonehenge.

8   It was a classic _voyage_ – flight, bus, hotel, everything included.

9   We're planning a long _outing_ across the Pyrenees, taking tents and everything with us.

10   A guided _tour_ of Manchester? How exciting!

11   In 1953 a British / New Zealand team set out on an historic _expn_ to conquer the world's greatest mountain, Everest.

12   Your _itinr_ will include two days in the Masai Mara reserve, where you will see lions, rhinos and lots of other spectacular wildlife.

All the words in the list are countable except *travel*. That means that *travel* has no plural form, and cannot take the indefinite article *a* or *an*. It is used when talking about the general idea rather than a particular trip. For example, there is a proverb *Travel broadens the mind*. Do you agree with this proverb?

# 3 Anagrams

Change the words in bold type so that the sentences make sense. Each of the words is an anagram of the correct word.

**1** Your knowledge of computer spreadsheets will be a big **seats** ( __*asset*__ ) in this job.

**2** So, your relationship is going through a difficult period? Perhaps **bedroom** ( _____ ) is the problem, and you both need change and development.

**3** They **design** ( _____ ) the contract, so it's a bit late to change their minds now.

**4** The trouble is that you often **laid** ( _____ ) the wrong number.

**5** Do I detect a **thin** ( _____ ) of jealousy in your tone?

**6** He was a man of very strong **ladies** ( _____ ), but sadly he often failed to live up to them.

**7** Now I know that you **idle** ( _____ ) about everything. I feel used and deceived. I hate you.

**8** She remained interested in politics. After she became blind, she read everything in **liberal** ( _____ ) she could lay her hands on.

**9** Which would you prefer – the scenic **outer** ( _____ ), or the more direct one taking the inner ring-road?

**10** She wore a pretty cotton trouser suit, pale yellow with thin black **priests** ( _____ ).

**11** He was angry that we failed to discuss the wide **anger** ( _____ ) of issues that he had raised in his report.

**12** I want to study **remain** ( _____ ) biology at university, because I love the sea.

**13** It's a sort of theme restaurant. There's poetry on the walls, and the menu is written in **serve** ( _____ ).

**14** This analysis shows up **reveals** ( _____ ) problems with our accounting system which will have to be sorted out.

**15** Claudia **spider** ( _____ ) herself on her ability to handle insects and other creepy-crawlies without any fear whatsoever.

Crossword clues in newspapers are often in the form of anagrams. For example: *the **master** is mixed up about this small river* is a clue for *stream*. Could you solve this clue: *there is something unsafe in the **garden**?* Check out Test 30 for more practice with mixed up letters.

# 4 Phrasal verbs 1

Replace the words in brackets using a suitable phrasal verb from the box. Put the verb in the correct form.

> come up with    drop in    get at    get down    get round    give away
> ~~go off~~    go out    go back    hand in    pass away    turn down

1    Some idiot turned off the fridge, and the milk has __gone__ __off__ . (*become sour*)

2    He looked quite convincing dressed as a woman, but his moustache _____ him _____ . (*revealed the truth about him*)

3    The game of chess originates from India and _____ _____ about two thousand years. (*is two thousand years old*)

4    I need a break. All this non-stop work is _____ me _____ . (*depressing*)

5    What exactly are you _____ _____ ? Have I done something wrong? (*trying to say*)

6    No, darling, it looks terrible. I think you'll find that purple spiky hair _____ _____ decades ago. (*became unfashionable*)

**7** I was offered a great job in America, but I had to _____ it _____ because I'm looking after my mother. (*refuse*)

**8** I know you're busy, but can't you just _____ _____ for a minute and say hello to the guys? (*visit briefly*)

**9** She's brilliant. We spent weeks on this software problem, getting nowhere. Then she arrived and _____ _____ a solution straightaway. (*thought of*)

**10** How can we _____ _____ the problem of over-staffing without actually sacking people? (*solve*)

**11** It's too late to change your mind now. You've _____ _____ your resignation. (*submitted*)

**12** After my husband _____ _____ I was grief stricken for years – well, weeks anyway. (*died*)

Many phrasal verbs have a number of meanings. Often they have a basic meaning and then one or more idiomatic uses. For example, *get down* can mean simply *climb* or *walk* or *jump* down; then there is the idiom *get down to work* meaning *start working seriously*; then there is the meaning in this test (which you have to work out for yourself!) Check out Test 21 for more practice with phrasal verbs.

# 5 Describing people

Describe the people below using adjectives from the box.

> clumsy    cynical    dynamic    elegant    genuine    gullible
> illiterate    intellectual    intimidating    skilful    superstitious
> tolerant    tough    ~~versatile~~    weird

1 Dustin Hoffman can take on almost any kind of role – comic,
  tragic, bizarre characters, everything. ___*versatile*___

2 My daughter believes absolutely everything you tell her. But she's
  only five. _____

3 My grandfather can't read or write. He worked on the family farm
  from the age of seven. _____

4 In my family we say that my brother has two left hands. He
  breaks everything. _____

5 My wife only wears designer clothes, and they look perfect on
  her. _____

6 My mother is a thinker, always discussing issues and reading.

  _____

7 My brother-in-law makes beautiful furniture. It's great to watch
  him working. _____

**8**  My aunt spends her life reading horoscopes, she carries lucky charms around with her, and she never, ever walks under a ladder! _____

**9**  My father is an old-style communist, but he seems to get on with everybody, whatever their politics. _____

**10**  My niece is a bit strange. She goes around wearing all black clothes and purple lipstick. She listens to old heavy metal bands. _____

**11**  My sister-in-law has had lots of trouble in her life, but she survives – and nobody pushes her around. _____

**12**  With my uncle, 'what you see is what you get'. He never says anything unless he means it, and he really cares about people. _____

**13**  My eldest son is always creating something. He's full of energy. _____

**14**  My cousin Vinnie always suspects everyone's motives. _____

**15**  My godmother has terribly strong views on things, and not many people dare to contradict her. _____

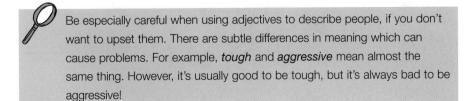

Be especially careful when using adjectives to describe people, if you don't want to upset them. There are subtle differences in meaning which can cause problems. For example, *tough* and *aggressive* mean almost the same thing. However, it's usually good to be tough, but it's always bad to be aggressive!

# 6 Parts of the body

Label the pictures with the correct words.

armpit    artery    calf    ~~eyelash~~    eyelid    heart    iris    kidney
knuckle    liver    lung    nostril    palm    pupil    ribs    shin
skull    sole    spine    thigh    vein

1    _eyelash_

2    _____

3    _____

4    _____

5    _____

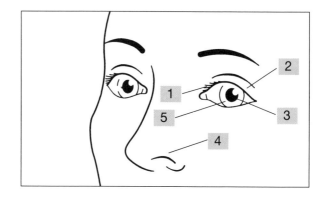

6    _____

7    _____

8    _____

9    _____

10    _____

11    _____

12    _____

13    _____

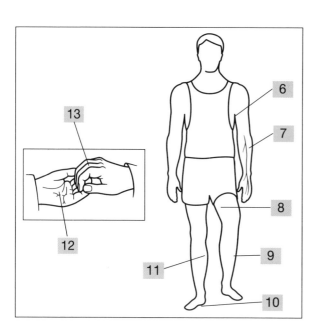

14 _____

15 _____

16 _____

17 _____

18 _____

19 _____

20 _____

21 _____

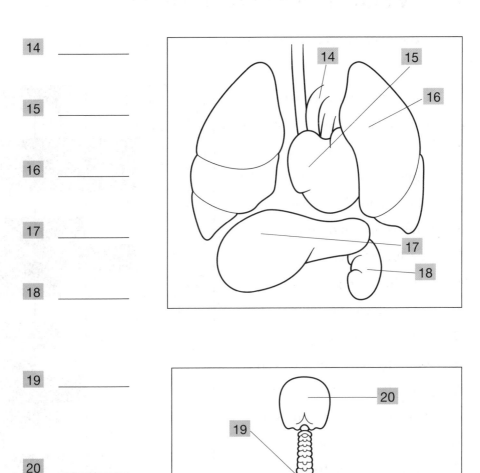

Parts of the body are one of the richest sources of idioms: *She didn't bat an eyelid* means she didn't react to something shocking. *Spineless* means *cowardly, lacking in courage*. And there are lots of idioms with the word *heart*. Do you know any?

# 7 Word association

The four words in each group have something in common. What are they all connected with?

|  |  | | | | | | | | | |
|---|-------|---|---|---|---|---|---|---|---|---|
| 1 | cell, warder, sentence, bars | P | R | I | S | O | N | | | |
| 2 | column, circulation, tabloid, article | | | W | | | | P | | |
| 3 | mattress, head, foot, sheet | B | | | | | | | | |
| 4 | bonnet, mirror, speedometer, fan | | A | | | | | | | |
| 5 | zodiac, moon, Mars, Sagittarius | A | | | R | | | | | Y |
| 6 | hand, strap, wind, time | | | T | | | | | | |
| 7 | paw, fur, whiskers, claws | | A | | | | | | | |
| 8 | lens, shutter, digital, flash | C | | | R | | | | | |
| 9 | wing, tail, engine, flight deck | | E | | | L | | | | |
| 10 | frame, glass, cleaner, break | | | N | O | | | | | |
| 11 | coffin, flowers, cemetery, corpse | F | | | | A | | | | |
| 12 | pawn, castle, bishop, queen | | H | | | | | | | |
| 13 | moat, walls, tower, dungeon | | | T | L | | | | | |
| 14 | corner, penalty, pass, transfer | | O | | | | L | | | |
| 15 | cowshed, tractor, barn, harvest | | | M | | | | | | |

It's not difficult to make sets of words like these for your friends to do. Just think of a theme, such as *hotel*, *doctor*, or *garden*; then write down four associated words. But try not to make them too easy!

# 8 Opposites crossword

Read the clues and complete the crossword.

**Across**

1 opposite of permanent (9)

4 opposite of professional (7)

6 opposite of trusting (10)

10 opposite of reliable (10)

11 opposite of compulsory (9)

**Down**

1 opposite of opaque (11)

2 opposite of precisely, exactly (13)

3 opposite of mean (8)

5 opposite of vertical (10)

7 opposite of junior (6)

8 opposite of inferior (8)

9 opposite of sharp (5)

 Some words have two 'opposites': *intelligent – unintelligent / stupid; honest – dishonest / deceitful.* There is usually a difference between the two. For example, as an opposite of *expensive, inexpensive* is much more polite than *cheap!*

# 9 Green issues

Complete the sentences using words from the box.

> biodiversity    conservation    consumption    erosion
> exhaust    exploitation    fertilizer    ~~food chain~~
> genetically modified (GM)    hydroelectric    pesticide
> rechargeable    renewable    residues    wind turbine

**1** Poisons which are used on one species can enter the
_food chain_ and affect other species.

**2** A chemical _____ may destroy harmful insects, but it
often has undesirable side-effects.

**3** A great deal of _____ is used to increase the yield of
crops. But it then runs off into the water supply and causes other
problems.

**4** Your car _____ may look OK, but in fact it is part of the
biggest and fastest growing global source of pollution.

**5** It is important to preserve as many species of plant and animal as
we can, to maintain _____ .

**6** Most of the wildlife of a country like Britain has long been
destroyed. The priority now is the _____ of what
remains.

**7** Conservationists are very suspicious of _____ crops;
they fear 'genetic pollution' of other species.

**8** A _____ produces totally clean energy. But some people think they are too big, noisy and ugly.

**9** Oil can only be used once, whereas _____ sources of energy like wind and the sun go on for ever.

**10** Where there are mountains and rainfall, _____ energy is often a good option.

**11** The use of _____ batteries, for example in personal stereos, helps to reduce waste and pollution.

**12** Most fruit and vegetables need to be washed carefully, as they carry pesticide _____ on their skins.

**13** The _____ of energy is very high in the rich, developed countries.

**14** In many places the destruction of forest has lead to serious _____ of the soil, and sometimes to flooding.

**15** The _____ of the world's natural resources has to be carefully managed.

A few years ago only scientists used the word *biodiversity*. Now politicians and the public use it as though they had known it all their lives. As green issues rise to the top of the agenda, green vocabulary enters everyday language. Learn it now and be ahead of the game!

# 10 Word building

Use the word on the right to make a new word which fits in the sentence.

1   He was born blind; but he has always treated
    this so-called ___disability___ as a challenge.                    **ABLE**

2   I'm _____ in favour of the plan, but there are
    still one or two points that I'm not entirely happy with.          **BASE**

3   Andrea does lovely paintings, photographs and
    drawings. She's just very _____ .                         **ART**

4   I think it's very _____ of the supervisor to
    expect us to work overtime every night this week.                  **REASON**

5   There is a saying in English: ' _____ speak
    louder than words.'                                                **ACT**

6   That rule is not _____ in this case.                      **APPLY**

7   Look at Chinese, Russian or Arabic. I think
    English is a _____ easy language to learn.                **COMPARE**

8   On no account repeat to anyone else what you
    have heard in this meeting. Treat it all as
    strictly _____ .                                          **CONFIDE**

**9**   I don't think their marriage will last long.
They're _____ quarrelling.      **CONTINUE**

**10**   You are now in our hands, Mr Bond. Do exactly
as you are told – _____ is punishable by
instant death.      **OBEY**

**11**   The lives of people in every country in the world
are being affected by economic _____ .      **GLOBAL**

**12**   He was extremely _____ . I had to do
everything myself.      **HELP**

**13**   He won silver in the discus at the Olympic Games
but was _____ after a drugs test.      **QUALIFY**

**14**   Industrial robots work with far greater _____
than any human.      **PRECISE**

**15**   You make these trivial incidents sound so _____ .
     **DRAMA**

It has become very common to make a verb by adding *-ize* to an adjective
(*modernize, trivialize, privatize*) or to a noun (*hospitalize, televize,*
*computerize*). You can then usually make an abstract noun like *privatization*
or *computerization*.

# 11 Ways of looking

Complete the sentences using words from the box. Put the words in the correct form.

> ~~catch a glimpse of~~    catch someone's eye    distinguish    glance
> look    notice    observe    peer    recognize    watch

1   I only _caught a glimpse of_ him, so I can't remember the colour of his clothes. He was white and clean-shaven. That's about it.

2   Actually I'm partly colour-blind, so I find it difficult  to _____ between similar colours.

3   _____ at me, Mummy! I'm on the table.

4   Are you going to _____ the Eddie Murphy film on TV tonight?

5   I kept trying to order, but the waiter was so busy that it was very difficult to _____ .

6   I was looking smart, and I joked loudly with my friends. I kept looking in her direction. But she didn't even _____ me.

7   She _____ at the empty chair for a moment, then carried on sorting the letters with tears in her eyes.

8   She'd changed so much, I hardly _____ her. She's completely lost her figure, poor thing.

9   The old man _____ through a gap in the closed curtains at his new neighbours.

10   'I've been _____ your behaviour for some time,' the police officer said. 'What exactly are you planning to do with fifteen paint spray cans and a ladder?'

The verb *look* itself has different uses, especially in phrasal verb combinations: *look up, look after, look forward to, look out.* Do you know any more?

# 12 Collective nouns

What are the collective nouns for these things? Complete the words in the grid.

| # | Clue | | | | | | | | | | | | |
|---|------|---|---|---|---|---|---|---|---|---|---|---|---|
| 1 | birds | F | L | O | C | K | | | | | | | |
| 2 | grapes | B | | | | | | | | | | | |
| 3 | actors in a play | | | | T | | | | | | | | |
| 4 | people | | R | | | | | | | | | | |
| 5 | cattle | H | | | | | | | | | | | |
| 6 | bees | | | A | | | | | | | | | |
| 7 | wolves | | | | K | | | | | | | | |
| 8 | fish | | H | | | | | | | | | | |
| 9 | directors | B | | | | | | | | | | | |
| 10 | ships | | | E | | | | | | | | | |
| 11 | cards | P | | | | | | | | | | | |
| 12 | thieves | | | | G | | | | | | | | |
| 13 | flowers | | | | | H | | | | | | | |
| 14 | antique coins | | | L | L | | | | | | | | |
| 15 | golf clubs | | E | | | | | | | | | | |

Collective nouns are a popular topic in textbooks for primary schools in Britain, especially the more unusual ones like *a school of whales, a pride of lions, a coven of witches, a gaggle of geese (on land)* and *a skein of geese (in the air).*

# 13 The kitchen

Write the number of the picture next to the correct word.

aluminium foil __11__     colander _____          kitchen towel _____

apron _____              draining board _____    rolling pin _____

carton _____             electric whisk _____    sieve _____

chopping board _____     food processor _____    timer _____

cling film _____         grater _____            wok _____

 All over the English-speaking world there is a keen interest in international cuisine – Italian, Greek, Indian, French and Chinese among others. So words like *ravioli, hummus, popadum, entrecote* and *wok* have entered the language.

# 14 Prepositions 1

Complete the sentences with prepositions.

**1** Giant pandas rarely breed _in_ captivity.

**2** My car's not worth much – ____ most £1,500 – but the insurance is still very expensive.

**3** ____ general, it's easier to learn computer skills from a person rather than from a book.

**4** What would you do if I sang ____ tune? Would you stand up and walk out on me?

**5** I don't know why they got married. They have absolutely nothing ____ common. Still, maybe that's what they like about each other.

**6** Can you believe that ____ average the English drink 3.25 cups of tea per person per day?

**7** Oh, what's the word? I know it, really! It's ____ the tip of my tongue!

**8** Salaries of $1 million are ____ no means unusual on Wall Street.

**9** Thank you for your interest in our company. We will file your CV and contact you ____ due course.

**10** Almost all the early jazz musicians played ____ ear. Art Tatum was classically trained, but he was an exception.

**11** The rent is to be paid ____ advance.

**12** His name is Leonardo, or Leo ____ short.

**13** This book is ____ far the best he's ever written.

**14** Work on the new software project is already ____ progress. It's a bit late to change the structure of it now.

**15** You resent this now, but it will be best for you ____ the long run, I feel sure.

Check out Test 31 for more practice with prepositions.

# 15 Cartoons 1

Write the correct letter under each cartoon.

a   Are you sure it's a goldfish, Ben?

b   I think perhaps you're overdoing the banana diet, Mr Mulholland.

c   Listen, darling, they're playing our tune.

d   Yes, but you want to be famous for what, exactly?

e   There must be an easier way to kill them, Paul.

f   Now they're all jealous of me because I conquered my paranoia.

1

_____b_____

2

_____

3

_____

4

_____

5

_____

6

_____

# 16 Who's the boss?

Choose the correct leader, top person or manager from the box on the right.

| # | | | |
|---|---|---|---|
| 1 | a TV programme | _producer_ | admiral |
| 2 | the United Nations | _____ | captain |
| 3 | a group of manual workers | _____ | chair |
| 4 | a shop | _____ | chef |
| 5 | a school | _____ | chief executive |
| 6 | kitchen staff | _____ | conductor |
| 7 | a football team | _____ | consultant |
| 8 | a museum | _____ | curator |
| 9 | a college | _____ | director |
| 10 | a committee | _____ | editor |
| 11 | a university | _____ | foreman |
| 12 | a company | _____ | governor |
| 13 | an orchestra | _____ | head teacher |
| 14 | a republic | _____ | manager |
| 15 | a newspaper or magazine | _____ | president |
| 16 | a prison | _____ | principal |
| 17 | a fleet of ships in the navy | _____ | ~~producer~~ |
| 18 | a film crew | _____ | Secretary General |
| 19 | a team of doctors | _____ | spokesperson |
| 20 | a group of protestors | _____ | vice chancellor |

In recent years management has become the subject of university courses, countless books and endless discussion. So it is not surprising that the traditional titles of managers have changed. The *managing director* has become the *chief executive*. *Heads of departments* are sometimes renamed *team leaders*, and new words like *facilitator* have come in. Even if the job is the same, the old *Personnel Manager* feels much better being called the *Human Resources Team Leader*!

# 17 Words for numbers

Read the definitions and complete the words on the grid.

1. A mythological animal with one horn.

| U | N | I | C | O | R | N |
|---|---|---|---|---|---|---|

2. A period of two weeks.

|  |  |  |  |  | G |  |
|---|---|---|---|---|---|---|

3. A combat between two people.

|  | U |  |  |
|---|---|---|---|

4. Able to use both hands equally well.

| A |  |  |  | D |  | X |  |  |  |  |  |
|---|---|---|---|---|---|---|---|---|---|---|---|

5. Two small telescopes joined together.

|  |  | N |  |  |  |  |  | S |
|---|---|---|---|---|---|---|---|---|

6. A match with two teams of two tennis players.

|  |  |  | B |  |  |  |
|---|---|---|---|---|---|---|

7. Two babies born at the same time.

|  | W |  |  |  |
|---|---|---|---|---|

8. Three babies born at the same time.

| T |  |  |  | L |  |  |  |
|---|---|---|---|---|---|---|---|

9. Four musicians playing together.

|  |  | A |  |  |  | T |  |
|---|---|---|---|---|---|---|---|

10. A five-sided figure.

|  |  |  | T |  | G |  |  |
|---|---|---|---|---|---|---|---|

11. System in which 'five' is written 101.

| B |  |  |  | R |  |
|---|---|---|---|---|---|

12. A period of ten years.

|  | E |  | A |  |  |
|---|---|---|---|---|---|

13. A period of a hundred years.

|  |  | N |  |  |  | Y |
|---|---|---|---|---|---|---|

14. A period of a thousand years.

|  | I |  |  |  |  |  | U |  |
|---|---|---|---|---|---|---|---|---|

15. 1,000,000 bytes (approximately).

|  |  |  |  | B | Y |  |  |
|---|---|---|---|---|---|---|---|

 You may find in your dictionary that a *billion* means *1,000,000,000* in the USA and *1,000,000,000,000* in Britain. This is no longer true. As they often do, the British have fallen in line with American use. Well, someone had to change, as this kind of confusion could be dangerous. You need to do two things: one, learn that *a billion means a thousand million*; two, throw away your old dictionary and get a new one.

# 18 Confusing words

Underline the correct word in each sentence.

1   The dress is a bit loose around the waist, but it shouldn't cost much to have it (*changed*/*altered*).

2   She clapped her hands gently in front of the baby's little face, and he (*blinked*/*winked*).

3   My brother is doing (*electrical*/*electric*) engineering at university.

4   Why don't you grow up, Dan? You're so (*childish*/*childlike*) sometimes.

5   There's a (*rumour*/*reputation*) going round the office that Anita and Steve are not just colleagues any more.

6   After the recession, there will be a period of growth. That is how the economic (*circle*/*cycle*) works.

7   South Wales was once a flourishing coal-mining area, but now there are hundreds of (*misused*/*disused*) coal mines in the valleys.

**8** My uncle is not actually a psychiatrist, but he's working as a (*councillor/counsellor*).

**9** It's hot. Let's go and sit in the (*shadow/shade*) for a while.

**10** I can see you next week – (*eventually/possibly*) on Friday, OK?

**11** The tennis match was held up for five minutes as the young Australian argued with the (*umpire/referee*).

**12** Have you any idea about the present government's (*politics/policy*) on third world debt? I don't think **they** have!

**13** His (*financial/economic*) worries were solved rather dramatically when he won £2 million on the National Lottery.

**14** England's World Cup campaign is not going well. But all the criticism in the press has not helped the (*morals/morale*) of the team.

**15** My new flat is just around the corner from the office, which is very (*convenient/comfortable*) for me.

 The prefix *mis-*, as in question 7, does not simply form a negative like *un-*. It always bears a meaning of something wrong or incorrect. The commonest example is, of course, *mistake*. Whereas *undiagnosed* means 'not noticed by the doctor', *misdiagnosed* means 'the doctor said it was food poisoning but in fact it was appendicitis'. Think about the differences between these pairs of words: *unguided / misguided; unheard / misheard; uninformed / misinformed; unmatched / mismatched.*

# 19 Film and TV

Write in the programme type or film genre.

| TV programme types | | Film genres | |
|---|---|---|---|
| documentary | chat show | cartoon | ~~comedy~~ |
| soap | wildlife programme | horror | romance |
| | | sci-fi | war film |

**1**  *Police School IV* (1993)
Those crazy cops go back to school again – with
hilarious results. The boys (and girls) in blue keep
up a high-speed chase – for jokes! More people
end up in custard than in custody!                    *comedy*

**2**  *Alfred Square* (6.05pm LWT)
Will Darren get out of his 'spot of bother' with the
police? Will Pam finally tell her boyfriend what is
going on behind his back? And will the feuding
sisters make it up? Find out in tonight's episode.    _____

**3**  *Aladdin's Magic Carpet* (2001)
A magical ride through the minarets of old Arabia.
Brilliant animation, gorgeous original music and the
voices of some of Hollywood's top stars.              _____

**4**  *Losing Colonel Brian* (1986)
A platoon of daring US soldiers go behind enemy lines
in Vietnam. Not all of them make it back to base.     _____

**5**  *Spring on the Wing* (8.30pm BBC 2)
Follow the great annual migration of birds from
southern Africa to Europe. Having undergone
thousands of miles of hardship, many are shot
for sport before they reach their destination.        _____

6 *The Silence of the Sheep* (1999)
A series of killings remains unexplained – until our pretty young heroine tracks down a man who prefers humans to hamburgers. Don't watch this on your own. Or better still, just don't watch it! _____

7 *On the Sofa* (9.30pm Channel 4)
Mike Parkins applies his charm to another glittering line-up of celebrities. Tonight's guests include Leonardo DiCaprio, supermodel Gabrielle and singer Craig David. _____

8 *Alien Website* (2002)
Outer space meets cyberspace as beings from the Andromeda galaxy take control of the Internet. Captain Spark and his crew are sent out on the hardest mission of their lives – to sort out the 'bugs'. _____

9 *One Enchanted Evening* (1949)
This still brings a tear to the eye, as we follow a lonely American GI and a beautiful French girl through 1940s Paris. Watch out for the kiss on top of the Eiffel Tower. _____

10 *The World in Focus* (10.45pm BBC 1)
Tonight's programme looks at the economics of renewable energy. Will it ever be possible to do without oil and gas? How much is Britain doing to develop wind and solar energy? _____

# 20 'She explained' and variations

Put the following words into the correct sentences. Use each word only once.

> boasted    complained    demanded    explained
> ~~insisted~~    lisped    pleaded    repeated    sighed
> stammered    whispered    yelled

1   'Oh, but you can't go yet. You really must stay for dinner,' she
      __insisted__ .

2   'Is anybody there?' The silence was only broken by the wind in
      the trees. 'Is anybody there?' she _____ .

3   'Don't waste my time. Where have you hidden the drugs?'
      _____ the policeman.

4   'Come on you reds!' _____ the crowd, as Arsenal closed in
      for a second goal.

**5**   'I love you, Darren,' she _____ ,pushing the dark curls away from his ear.

**6**   'I have to admit that I'm really brilliant at art and science and music. Oh, and sport,' she _____ .

**7**   'W... w ... would you mind terribly if I k... k... k.... kissed you?' he _____ .

**8**   'The company's cash-flow crisis makes it impossible to keep you all,' _____ the spokesperson. 'There will be job losses, I'm afraid.'

**9**   'Please don't kill my husband!' _____ a tearful woman, as the government soldiers lined a group of captured rebels against a wall.

**10**  'This pasta is cold, and the sauce is too salty,' she _____ to the waiter. 'Have you got anything edible on the menu?'

**11**  'Yeth, that ith very pretty,' the little girl _____ .

**12**  'Ah, well,' he _____ . 'That's the end of that, I suppose. It was nice while it lasted.'

Long passages of dialogue can be very repetitive if you keep using *he said, she said* over and over again. So exploit the words in this test to liven up your writing, and add variety. In speech, they are more commonly without quotes: *we complained about the rudeness of the staff* or with indirect forms: *she insisted that we should eat with them.*

# 21 Phrasal verbs 2

Complete the sentences with a phrasal verb from the box. Put the verb into the correct form.

> come round   cut out   fall apart   get out of   get round to
> get through to   go on about   go over   go through with   ~~let off~~
> put off   put on   put up   put up with   work out

1   She was doing over 70mph in a 30mph area, but she smiled sweetly at the policeman and he ___let___ her ___off___ .
    (*didn't charge her*)

2   This is madness. I don't even fancy him, and now we're getting married. I can't _____ it.
    (*carry on and actually do it*)

3   When he _____ after the accident, he couldn't recognise any of us. It was really worrying.
    (*regained consciousness*)

4   I'm not very fussy, but I simply can't _____ that wallpaper any longer. One of us will have to go.  (*tolerate, bear*)

5   Let's _____ these figures again, shall we? They just don't seem to add up.  (*examine*)

6   I've been meaning to reply to her e-mail, but I just haven't _____ it yet. Maybe I never will!
    (*found the time to do*)

7   Don't buy a cheap bike. They _____ in weeks.
    (*get broken easily*)

**8** _____ the sales talk. Just tell me your lowest price. (*omit, don't give me*)

**9** I promised to go to their boring party, and now it's very hard to _____ it. (*escape from the commitment*)

**10** I'm going to be in Washington for two days. I wondered if you could _____ me _____ ? (*let me stay in your flat*)

**11** I don't like going to the dentist – who does? So I've been _____ it _____ . (*delaying, postponing*)

**12** You've changed so much. I can't seem to _____ you any more. (*communicate with*)

**13** My girlfriend _____ every day, but I prefer eating and watching TV. (*does exercise, goes to the gym*)

**14** She's not really upset, you know. She's _____ it _____ for your benefit. (*pretending, faking*)

**15** Oh, don't _____ your digital camera again. We all know it's brilliant. (*keep talking*)

In relative clauses, what do you do with all these prepositions? Do we say: *That's the number through to which I couldn't get?* No, definitely not. Everybody says: *That's the number I couldn't get through to.* Winston Churchill was once criticized for putting prepositions at the end of a sentence, and his reply was, 'This is the sort of English up with which I will not put.' (This, in case you don't know, sounds ridiculous.) Check out Test 4 for more practice with phrasal verbs.

# 22 Which horse won the race?

Here are the horses and betting odds for the 2.15pm race at Kempton Park:

| Horse | Betting odds |
|---|---|
| SIMPLY RED | 25–1 |
| FISH 'N' CHIPS | 2–1 (Favourite) |
| EMERALD ISLE | 10–1 |
| MISS PIGGY | 5–1 |
| CYBER BABE | 10–1 |
| FLIRTATIOUS | 10–1 |
| LOTTERY LASS | 50–1 |
| DOT COM | 50–1 |

Now read through these sentences and see if you can work out who came 1st, 2nd and 3rd.

Flirtatious was in the lead with 400 metres to go.
There were only six finishers.
The horse that came second was an outsider (more than 20–1)
Lottery Lass came last.
The favourite was in the lead with only 200 metres to go.
The winning horse had odds of 10–1.
Simply Red fell at the third jump.
Miss Piggy passed the favourite 100 metres from the finish.
Cyber Babe did not finish the race.
Flirtatious came 5th.

1st _____ _____   2nd _____ _____   3rd _____ _____

There are quite a few idioms from the world of horse racing and betting: *jockeying for position; to win by a nose; to fall at the first hurdle; to spur on; a dark horse; neck and neck.* If you can't work out the meanings of any of these, look them up.

# 23 Add two letters

Add two letters to each of the following words to form a new word.

| | | | | |
|---|---|---|---|---|
| 1 | sit | → | _sixth_ | : not fifth |
| 2 | dead | → | _____ | : ten years |
| 3 | way | → | _____ | : tired of life |
| 4 | lay | → | _____ | : tall and thin |
| 5 | ripe | → | _____ | : read this and cook |
| 6 | dear | → | _____ | : dull, boring, colourless |
| 7 | come | → | _____ | : what you earn |
| 8 | rug | → | _____ | : a bit like American football |
| 9 | seen | → | _____ | : the picture is on this part of the TV |
| 10 | tend | → | _____ | : make something longer, in time or space |
| 11 | tray | → | _____ | : what traitors do |
| 12 | cell | → | _____ | : keep your wine in this |
| 13 | shop | → | _____ | : a top person in the church |
| 14 | red | → | _____ | : have babies |
| 15 | close | → | _____ | : put something in the envelope |
| 16 | fit | → | _____ | : belief in god |
| 17 | light | → | _____ | : joy |
| 18 | gap | → | _____ | : hold tight, or understand |
| 19 | miner | → | _____ | : type of drinking water – fizzy or still |
| 20 | sign | → | _____ | : give up the job |

# 24 Crime and punishment

Complete the sentences using words from the box.

| | | | | | | | |
|---|---|---|---|---|---|---|---|
| arrest | bail | charge | committed | court | ~~defence~~ | evidence | fine |
| juvenile | lawyer | prosecution | prove | sentence | verdict | witness | |

1  The __*defence*__ lawyer said that his client didn't intend to cause injury.

2  Drop the gun. That's better. Now – you are under _____ .

3  I know my rights. I want to phone my _____ .

4  The prosecution says that my client stole millions of pounds via the internet. But where is the _____ ?

5  The _____ of this court is 'guilty'. Have you anything to say?

6  Everyone knew the woman was 100% guilty, but they just couldn't _____ it.

7  I now call my next _____ , Mrs McPherson, the defendant's mother-in-law.

8  You are a rich man, and just paying a _____ will not punish you enough. I am going to send you to prison. Let this be a lesson to you.

9  Officer, you have arrested my client. Now you must either
   _____ her or let her go.

10  For those under 16 there is a special _____ court.

11  The Appeal Court might reduce your _____ from four
    years to, say, three. But they can also increase it.

12  You can deposit £50,000 with the court, and be released on
    _____ . But if you disappear, you will lose the money. Do
    you understand that?

13  If your defence lawyer is better than the _____ lawyer,
    you may get off.

14  This wicked man has _____ the most appalling crimes,
    and all decent people will agree that he should receive a very long
    prison sentence indeed.

15  Be in _____ at 9.30. The hearing begins at 10 o'clock, and
    the magistrates don't like to be kept waiting.

The legal system in Britain seems very old-fashioned. The judges and
lawyers still wear black gowns and white wigs. Lawyers have to address the
judge as *M'lud* (= My Lord). So you will not be surprised that the language
of the law is also rather antique, with very long sentences and bits of French
and Latin thrown in.

# 25 IT and computers

Read the clues and complete the crossword.

## Across

1   Little label that looks like piano keys, and is read by the computer in the supermarket. (3, 4)

4   Use this type of program for maths and accounts – good for making charts. (11)

5   Abbreviation for 'Internet Service Provider'. (3)

7   Files are kept neat and tidy in one of these. (6)

9   Use a _____ program to write letters, reports – and poetry, if you like. (4,10)

11   This is used for storing and retrieving lots of addresses, book titles and things like that. (8)

12   Want to put an old photo into your computer? Use one of these. (7)

13   Ouch! You can lose all your data when computers _____ (5)

14   Correct word for the 'TV set' with your computer. (7)

## Down

2   You don't like wires messing up your desk? Get a _____ mouse. (8)

3   Use different _____ to make your text look nice. (5)

4   No good at spelling? Use one of these! (12)

6   You shouldn't buy _____ software – it's illegal. (7)

7   It's easy to _____ text on a computer (i.e. to change the font, colour, to add bold, italic etc.) (6)

8   To move text around, you can cut and _____ it. (5)

10   To put new software onto the computer. (7)

# 26 Classifications

First put the words in the box into the right lists. Then complete a group word for each list.

> abstract    ~~autumn~~    barrel    because    botany    etc.
> five eighths    in    cholera    methane    novelist    onyx
> rectangle    spreadsheet    swallow

1   spring, summer, __*autumn*__ , winter

2   carton, crate, _____ , can

3   triangle, circle, _____ , square

4   and, but, _____ , although

5   a half, two thirds, _____ , a twelfth

6   astronomy, biology, _____ , physics

7   Dr, e.g., _____ , approx.

8   amethyst, emerald, _____ , opal

9   ammonia, carbon dioxide, _____ , ether

10   vulture, pheasant, _____ , wren

11   over, after, _____ , by

12   malaria, tuberculosis, _____ , AIDS

13   poet, biographer, _____ , historian

14   portrait, landscape, _____ , still life

15   word processing, game, _____ , graphics

When you can't think of the right general word, it's perfectly normal to give a short list of examples. Not many people have the word *peripherals* in their everyday vocabulary, so they say *keyboards, printers, mice and so on.*

| # | 1 | 2 | 3 | 4 | 5 | 6 | 7 | 8 | 9 |
|---|---|---|---|---|---|---|---|---|---|
| 1 | S | E | A | S | O | N | S | | |
| 2 | C | | | | | | | R | |
| 3 | | | A | | | | | | |
| 4 | | | | J | | | T | | N |
| 5 | | R | | | I | | | | |
| 6 | S | | | N | | | | | |
| 7 | | B | B | | V | | T | | |
| 8 | G | | | | | | | | |
| 9 | | | S | | | | | | |
| 10 | | I | | | | | | | |
| 11 | | | | P | S | | I | | |
| 12 | D | | | A | | | | | |
| 13 | | | I | R | | | | | |
| 14 | P | | | T | | G | | | |
| 15 | | | | G | | M | | | |

# 27 From 'shore' to 'crash'

Change the word SHORE into CRASH in sixteen stages, changing one or two letters at a time. The number in brackets tells you how many letters to change.

| | S | H | O | R | E | |
|---|---|---|---|---|---|---|
| 1 | S | C | O | R | E | For example Man Utd 2 – Arsenal 0 (1) |
| 2 | | | | | | Frighten (1) |
| 3 | | | | | | You can play this on a piano (1) |
| 4 | | | | | | A large marine mammal (2) |
| 5 | | | | | | A conjunction (1) |
| 6 | | | | | | Body language for happiness (2) |
| 7 | | | | | | Odour (2) |
| 8 | | | | | | Quite hard to do correctly in English (1) |
| 9 | | | | | | Don't ____ children. Be strict. (2) |
| 10 | | | | | | A country in Europe (2) |
| 11 | | | | | | A means of transport (2) |
| 12 | | | | | | A tiny piece of sand (1) |
| 13 | | | | | | Make wine from this fruit (2) |
| 14 | | | | | | Cows do this in fields (1) |
| 15 | | | | | | Rub out (2) |
| 16 | C | R | A | S | H | (2) |

You can create one of these puzzles for friends. Start with a word of about five letters (very short and very long ones don't work). Keep changing letters to make new words until you end up with something completely different. Many words lead nowhere, unfortunately – it's just a matter of trial and error!

# 28 Odd one out

Underline the odd one out on the left and write it into the correct sentence on the right.

| | | | |
|---|---|---|---|
| 1 | bridegroom, photographer, reception, <u>modem</u> | a | A _____ is not an academic. |
| 2 | hepatitis, hypothesis, meningitis, psoriasis | b | A _____ is not a job. |
| 3 | harvest, instalment, mortgage, deposit | c | A _____ is not part of a car. |
| 4 | score, bass, chord, salmon | d | A *modem* has nothing to do with a wedding. |
| 5 | historian, physicist, hypnotist, philosopher | e | A _____ is not a form of literature. |
| 6 | bumper, heel, boot, gear | f | A _____ has nothing to do with the office. |
| 7 | mobile, handset, cordless, collarless | g | A _____ is not part of the body. |
| 8 | lens, syringe, shutter, tripod | h | A _____ has nothing to do with the police. |
| 9 | leisure, option, output, humble | i | A _____ is not an illness. |
| 10 | grocer, butler, miner, grater | j | _____ has nothing to do with phones. |
| 11 | throat, trout, rib, knuckle | k | A _____ has nothing to do with cameras. |
| 12 | pass, score, corner, skate | l | A _____ has nothing to do with money. |
| 13 | stationery, files, recipe, copier | m | _____ is an adjective, not a noun. |
| 14 | novel, navel, autobiography, poem | n | A _____ has nothing to do with music. |
| 15 | handcuffs, truncheon, tune, notebook | o | _____ has nothing to do with football. |

 The phrase *nothing to do with* ... is very common and useful. But the grammar that goes with it is a bit strange: you can say either *it **has** nothing do with biology* or *it **is** nothing to do with biology*.

# 29 Crawling and other ways of moving

Complete the sentences using words from the box.

| | | | | | |
|---|---|---|---|---|---|
| crawled | leapt | limped | loitered | plodded | skipped |
| | staggered | strolled | ~~stumbled~~ | tramped | |

1   The ground was rough, and I was an inexperienced climber.
    I _stumbled_ and fell down a crevasse, breaking both my legs.

2   The happy children _____ along the road to school.

3   By now mortally wounded, our heroine _____ into the
    smoke-filled barn to send one last radio message to her comrades.

4   They fixed his leg, but he _____ for the rest of his life.

5   The villain _____ casually past the car, but I saw him
    check out the phone inside.

6   Exhausted, and with her boots caked in mud, the vet
    _____ back to her car.

7   The thieves _____ around the front of the shop for ages
    before breaking in.

8   We _____ through miles of forest looking for mushrooms.

9   After all that, I just _____ into my sleeping-bag and went
    straight to sleep.

10  I was pleased to see that you all _____ out of bed when I
    set the fire alarm off. Just checking!

# 30 Mixed up letters

Rearrange the letters in bold type to make adjectives to complete the sentences.

**1**  Everything about this book is **burdisting** ( <u>  disturbing  </u> ) –
the characters, the events, the language. It actually upset me.

**2**  The battle scenes are not very **israltiec** ( _____ ),
despite all the computer imaging that has gone into them.

**3**  The story-line of this novel is totally **gingprip** ( _____ ),
– quite literally, I couldn't put it down.

**4**  This film provides a **scninatfaig** ( _____ ) insight into
the jazz scene of 1970s New York.

**5**  Another **luld** ( _____ ) little tale of middle-class
Londoners talking about each other. I'm tired of such novels.

**6**  Disability in movies can be sentimental. But this account of
one young boy's struggle with epilepsy is genuinely **vinmog**
( _____ ).

**7**  The film's images of bodies being taken over by a sort of
bubbling, steaming skin disease are **ferritingy** ( _____ ).

**8**  The acting of this young Hollywood star is, as always, mildly
**tatiriring** ( _____ ). I apologise to his many fans, but
he does get on my nerves.

**9**  The brushwork on this painting is delicate and **tiequisex**
( _____ ), reminding me rather of Watteau.

**10**  The exhibition is worth visiting just for the **gintriks**
( _____ ) installation by Tracey Emin. As you walk in,
it hits you right between the eyes.

# 31 Prepositions 2

Complete the sentences with the correct prepositions.

1  I love going away __on__ business and getting away from the family. They all drive me mad.

2  I don't understand anything on this Thai menu. I think I'll choose something _____ random.

3  Phone or send an e-mail. Keep _____ touch, anyway.

4  You want to go out with a guy in the office? Did you have anyone _____ mind, or do you like them all?

5  All those _____ favour _____ the proposal, please say yes now.

6  Lend you £2,000? You must be completely _____ your mind!

7  Actually, _____ second thoughts, I might be able to lend you the money. But you will have to do me a favour.

8  With credit cards and internet shopping, it's all too easy to get _____ debt.

9  Are you _____ good terms with your probation officer?

10  I know a nice little place _____ the outskirts of town. Will you join us?

**11**    This device is _____ the cutting edge of technology, you realize.

**12**    We're advertising it exclusively _____ our website.

**13**    Don't ask me about that son of mine; _____ all I know he is in an Australian prison by now.

**14**    The temperature in Egypt at the moment? Well, _____ a guess I'd say about 35 degrees. Pretty hot, in any case.

**15**    You tell me what's _____ offer, and I will tell you if I'm interested, OK?

Prepositions are among the most difficult bits of vocabulary to learn. They don't correspond very closely to prepositions in other languages, so they cause translation problems. It is not at all easy to sum up the 'meaning' of a word like *by*. We think first of its place use: *she's over there by the bar*. Then maybe of its use with agents: *he was chosen by the committee*. But there are also lots of phrases which don't fit into those two uses: *by night, bit by bit, by a long way, by name, by mistake* and *it's all right by me*. Check out Test 14 for more practice with prepositions.

# 32 Idioms

Complete the sentences using words from the box. Put the words into the correct form.

| | | |
|---|---|---|
| a level playing field | call it a day | can't make head or tail of |
| given the sack | go down like a lead balloon | have it in for |
| make a meal of it | ~~out of order~~ | out of the blue |
| pull your socks up | ring a bell | talking shop |

**1** You can't call off our date now – I've got the tickets and everything. That's totally __*out of order*__ . (*unacceptable*)

**2** I reckon we've done enough. Shall we _____ ? (*finish*)

**3** Why should I look on the bright side? I've just been _____ . (*dismissed from my job*)

**4** There's no point in you coming out with us. We'll only be _____ . (*discussing work*)

**5** We were all stunned. Completely _____ she said, 'I'm leaving Reggie. The thing is, I've fallen in love with another man.' (*very unexpectedly*)

**6** You'd better _____ , my girl. At your present work-rate, you're not going to get the grades you need. (*start working hard*)

**7** I'm afraid I _____ these video programming instructions. It's probably because I'm over 15. (*can't understand at all*)

**8** Jimmy 'the Bull' Gavrano. Now that name _____ ...
Wasn't he a New York mafia boss?
(*is somewhere hidden in my memory*)

**9** Look, don't _____. All I asked you to do was tidy up
some computer files, not rebuild my life for me.
(*make the job bigger than necessary*)

**10** I told that joke about the stupid policeman and it
_____ . It turned out that most of them at the
party were police trainees. (*got a very negative reaction*)

**11** I do my best, but for some reason or other my boss
_____ me. (*is hostile to*)

**12** This company is not asking for any special treatment. All we want
is _____ . (*the same fair deal as others*)

Idioms from the world of sport are popular even with people who don't
follow sport at all: *to score an own-goal, keep your eye on the ball, paddle
your own canoe, it's a knockout*. Which of the idioms in the test is
connected with sport? Check out Tests 39, 40 and 42 for more practice
with idioms.

# 33 The world of business and industry

Complete the sentences using words from the box.

> brand    corporate identity    economies of scale    flexible    forecast
> market forces    output    productivity    profit margins    restructure
> salaries    subsidiary    ~~takeover~~    training    wages

**1** A big German company is planning a ___*takeover*___ of British bicycle maker Rollo Ltd.

**2** In agriculture, _____ have been squeezed by higher fuel costs and increasing competition from imports.

**3** Failing internet giant, XZL.com will _____ its management, with the loss of dozens of executive jobs.

**4** The _____ of workers in our factory are below average, but they do receive other benefits.

**5** We plan to increase management _____ by 17% again this year, as we need to attract high quality applicants.

**6** The profit _____ for the next half year is almost $2 billion, which is quite healthy in the view of US analysts.

**7** Fizzycola is a wholly-owned _____ of Megacola, but enjoys much independence from the parent company.

**8**   Our emphasis this year will be investment in _____ .
We believe that the skills of the workforce are our greatest asset.

**9**   This company is very big and of course saves money through
_____ . But at the same time it is difficult to manage.

**10**   We want to see Krunch-Bar become the best-known
_____ in the chocolate snack market.

**11**   The new logo and colours on our publicity brochures are
important in establishing our _____ . We need to be
seen as fresh, young, dynamic – but at the same time committed
to quality.

**12**   Our prices are pushed up and down by _____ , as are
everyone else's. We have to work with that.

**13**   They are producing the same number of units as last year – in
other words, _____ has remained constant.

**14**   We have lost a lot of staff, but we are still achieving the same
output. So _____ has risen – that's the key to our
success.

**15**   Our workforce is now very _____ ; they will take on
different jobs and move from one plant to another.

# 34 Headlines

Match the newspaper headlines to the short extracts from the articles. Write the correct letter in the box.

1
*Audi-ya do it?*

c

2
Boost to under-18 team



3
**BROWN'S FUEL PEACE BID**



4
*CABINET BACKS EURO PLAN*



5
PM cuts health budget



6
*Poll gives lead to Greens*



7
Refugee tide warning



8
Top cop quits

**a**

The chancellor last night attempted to calm protests over petrol prices.

**b**

The Chief Constable of Greater Manchester has resigned.

**c**

A thief demonstrated yesterday how he could steal a locked car in less than 30 seconds. That's how long it took to break into a £30,000 German saloon.

**d**

'Actually such numbers are easily absorbed,' said a Home Office spokeswoman.

**e**

The trainee soccer players were encouraged by the £100,000 grant from the Sports Council.

**f**

'Winning this election is very important for us,' said Ms Thomson.

**g**

Spending on hospitals will be reduced by 1.5% over the next two years.

**h**

The proposals now enjoy the support of the government.

 Check out Tests 38 and 46 for more practice with error correction.

# 35 Animal parts

Label the pictures with the correct word from the box.

| | | | | | | | |
|---|---|---|---|---|---|---|---|
| beak | claws | feathers | fin | hoof | ~~mane~~ | paw | reins |
| saddle | scales | shoe | talons | trunk | tusk | whiskers | |

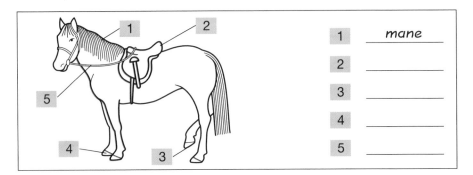

1 _mane_

2 _____

3 _____

4 _____

5 _____

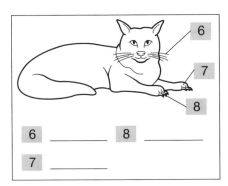

6 _____   8 _____

7 _____

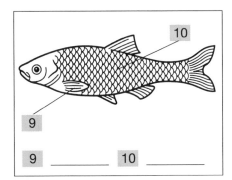

9 _____   10 _____

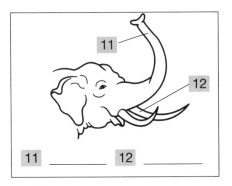

11 _____   12 _____

13 _____

14 _____

15 _____

 Check out Test 1 for more practice with animal words.

# 36 What is it part of?

Complete the sentences with a word from the column on the right.

| | | | | |
|---|---|---|---|---|
| 1 | A viewfinder is part of | _a camera_ | a | a needle |
| 2 | A frame is part of | _____ | b | a book |
| 3 | A pip is part of | _____ | c | a shoe |
| 4 | A neck is part of | _____ | d | a supermarket |
| 5 | An eye is part of | _____ | e | a computer |
| 6 | A petal is part of | _____ | f | a chair |
| 7 | A key is part of | _____ | g | a window |
| 8 | A pawn is part of | _____ | h | a piano |
| 9 | A twig is part of | _____ | i | a bottle |
| 10 | A beak is part of | _____ | j | a knife |
| 11 | An arm is part of | _____ | k | a sailing boat |
| 12 | A blade is part of | _____ | l | a~~camera~~ |
| 13 | A spine is part of | _____ | m | a chess set |
| 14 | A barrel is part of | _____ | n | a flower |
| 15 | A sole is part of | _____ | o | a petrol engine |
| 16 | A hard disk is part of | _____ | p | a rifle |
| 17 | A carburettor is part of | _____ | q | a bird |
| 18 | A video camera is part of | _____ | r | an orange |
| 19 | A mast is part of | _____ | s | a branch |
| 20 | A check-out is part of | _____ | t | a surveillance system |

# 37 Sickness and health

Complete the sentences using words from the box.

> allergic    anaesthetic    antibodies    ~~antiseptic~~
> crutches    dermatologist    diarrhoea    hay fever
> infectious    insomnia    maternity    midwife
> prescription    sedative    transfusion

1    It's only a scratch, but it could get dirty. Put some _antiseptic_ cream on it.

2    She was rushed to hospital in labour, but there was no room in the _____ ward, so she ended up in a general ward.

3    But in the end it was an easy birth, attended by a _____ . She didn't see a doctor until later.

4    I'm a tough guy. You can do that little operation without _____ . Ow! On second thoughts, can I change my mind about that?

5    Every summer I get really bad _____ . It's a shame, because I love gardens and the countryside.

6    In fact I'm _____ to all sorts of things – nuts, eggs, chocolate and loads more.

7    There was a delay in giving the _____ , as the hospital had no supplies of her blood group.

**8** Before an operation, they usually give you a _____ , which calms you down very nicely.

**9** This book is so boring that it should be sold as a cure for

_____ .

**10** I took the _____ to the chemist, but she couldn't read it and had phone my doctor to find out what it said!

**11** The whole family had _____ . The queue for the toilet was terrible.

**12** I've had some kind of 'flu. But don't worry – it's past the _____ stage by now.

**13** It's only a sprained ankle, but he's been walking around on _____ for ten days.

**14** This test doesn't actually find the virus; it checks for _____ in your system.

**15** I thought this spot might be skin cancer, but the _____ told me it was nothing serious.

 The names of medical specialists are similar in many languages, but the exact form – and the pronunciation – can be difficult to get right. Try saying these quickly three times – *anaesthetist, ophthalmologist, cardiologist, paediatrician, gynaecologist, obstetrician, psychiatrist!*

# 38 A badly written menu

The manager of this restaurant is not brilliant at English, and he has made sixteen mistakes in the menu. Underline them and correct them.

---

## Pasta

*parmesan* Lasagna with spinach

Spaghetti with <u>partisan</u> cheese and tomato source

Spaghetti with garlic and herbs

The Chef's Special Ravioli filled with tomato and him

## Meat

Veal in breadcrumbs

Perk cutlets

Wild Boer sausages

Venison stew

Lame chops

Scottish beef stake

## Chicken and Game

Roast peasant (shot locally)

Roast cartridge with orange sauce

Stir-fried organic chicken with ginger and garlic

## Fish

Grilled red mallet

Place in white wine sauce

Grilled tuner

Thai-style pawns in hot sauce

## Vegetables

Broccoli

Beens

Cabbage

Parrots

Pleas

---

Check out Tests 34 and 46 for more practice with error correction.

# 39 Idiomatic similes

Complete the similes using words from the box.

> a bat    a bee    brass    clockwork    a cucumber
> a daisy    ditchwater    a dodo    a feather    a fox    gold
> the grave    ~~a hatter~~    the hills    life    nails    a parrot
> a picture    a rock    toast

| | | | |
|---|---|---|---|
| **1** | As mad as _a hatter_ | **11** | As sick as _____ |
| **2** | As dead as _____ | **12** | As steady as _____ |
| **3** | As light as _____ | **13** | As pretty as _____ |
| **4** | As regular as _____ | **14** | As bold as _____ |
| **5** | As blind as _____ | **15** | As cool as _____ |
| **6** | As large as _____ | **16** | As warm as _____ |
| **7** | As dull as _____ | **17** | As old as _____ |
| **8** | As cunning as _____ | **18** | As fresh as _____ |
| **9** | As hard as _____ | **19** | As silent as _____ |
| **10** | As busy as _____ | **20** | As good as _____ |

These similes are all common idioms. But original similes are also much used by poets and comedians. Wordsworth's most famous opening lines are: *I wandered lonely as a cloud, That floats on high o'er vales and hills*. Check out Tests 32, 40 and 42 for more practice with idioms.

# 40 Animal idioms

Complete the sentences with the phrases below.

| | |
|---|---|
| big fish in a small pond | pecking order |
| chicken-feed | ~~ruffle feathers~~ |
| dinosaurs | teaching an old dog new tricks |
| empty nest | the cat that got the cream |
| fly on the wall | top dog |
| kill the goose that lays the golden eggs | barking up the wrong tree |
| loan shark | wild horses couldn't tear them apart |
| more fish in the sea | |

1   The appointment of Esther as office manager is going to
    __*ruffle feathers*__ . She's about 20 years younger than most
    of the staff.

2   My youngest sister has just left home and my poor parents are
    suffering from _____ syndrome.

3   Mick Jagger, David Bowie, Mick Fleetwood and a few other rock
    _____ will be playing at the show.

4   If possible, borrow the money from a proper bank. Don't go to
    some _____ who will charge you 75% interest,
    and then send a gangster round to collect the money.

5   All the lecturers in the department are officially equal, so there's a
    constant struggle over who's _____ .

6   Just accept that the neighbours had nothing to do with the death
    of your dog. You're _____ , if you'll excuse the pun.

7   In my small town I was a _____ . Now I'm in
    London, nobody has heard of me – I'm just one of thousands of
    DJs hanging round the music scene.

**8** You mustn't sell off the pizza delivery service – it's the most profitable part of the business. If you do, you will

_____ .

**9** Try to forget about that stupid guy, Alice. You're a lovely girl, and there are plenty _____ .

**10** Look, in this company you don't choose your afternoon off until the deputy manager has chosen hers, the supervisor has chosen his and I have chosen mine. There's a strict _____ .

**11** The work may be interesting and 'rewarding', but no-one does it for the money. The pay is _____ .

**12** Ever since the first day of term those two have been inseparable;

_____ .

**13** On TV there was an amazing _____ documentary about life behind the scenes in a police station. They didn't seem to realize the camera was there.

**14** Why the big, broad smile and the humming? You look like

_____ .

**15** You're a retired football coach, and this job involves a lot of computer skills. So it's a question of _____ . Are you sure you're up to it?

Check out Tests 32, 39 and 42 for more practice with idioms.

# 41 Travel and holidays

Which responses go with these sentences? Write the correct letter in the space.

1   Did you book, Madame? __e__

2   Do you know the exchange rate? _____

3   Do you have a complaint, sir? _____

4   Have you anything to declare? _____

5   How about a self-catering villa in Tunisia? _____

6   I reckon we should check in now. _____

7   Did you make an insurance claim? _____

8   Let's get a package holiday. _____

9   Have you registered, Madame? _____

10  Please proceed to baggage reclaim. _____

**a**  Isn't it a bit early? The flight's not for another two hours.

**b**  Yes. We got the full value of the camera and a bit for the damaged suitcase.

**c**  Will you do that while I try phoning? There are three cases, remember.

**d**  Just this bottle of perfume. Do I have to pay duty on it?

**e**  Yes. One double room for four days. The name is McIntosh.

**f**  Isn't that a bit unadventurous? I think it would be more fun to find hotels and transport when we get there – and it may be cheaper, too.

**g**  That's a great idea. Then we can get food from the market and take it in turns cooking.

**h**  Yes. It seems to be impossible to regulate the air-conditioning.

**i**  Yes. We signed in and left our passports with you this morning.

**j**  Yes. It's about 1.6 Swiss francs to the dollar.

When travelling, you often have to give your name and other information to people. It helps to spell out some words with the International Spelling Alphabet:

| | | | |
|---|---|---|---|
| Alpha | Hotel | Oscar | Victor |
| Bravo | India | Papa | Whisky |
| Charlie | Juliet | Quebec | X-ray |
| Delta | Kilo | Romeo | Yankee |
| Echo | Lima | Sierra | Zulu |
| Foxtrot | Mike | Tango | |
| Golf | November | Uniform | |

(This is what airline pilots use to avoid dangerous mistakes.)

# 42 Idioms – weather and nature

Complete the sentences with the idioms below. Where necessary, change the forms to fit the sentences.

| | |
|---|---|
| a drop in the ocean | freeze out |
| a huge outcry | go with the flow |
| landslide victory | find (your) roots |
| a storm in a teacup | ~~see the wood for the trees~~ |
| an uphill struggle | the calm before the storm |
| blown off course | get bogged down |

1   Stand back and look at the whole situation. You can't
    **see the wood for the trees** .
    (*can't get a general picture because you are confused by the detail*)

2   This project has been _____ all the way.
    (*a hard job without breaks*)

3   In the end I just gave up with Inger. She sort of _____ me
    _____ . (*was always unfriendly*).

4   I'm not going to be difficult about this. I'll just
    _____ .
    (*accept what everyone else has agreed*)

5   As a manager, you should make the big decisions. Don't
    _____ in the detail.
    (*become too involved*)

**6** We get a lot of Americans coming to Ireland to

_____ .

(*get information about their ancestors*)

**7** A million dollars may sound like a lot of money, but it's
_____ in this situation.
(*an insignificant amount*)

**8** Everyone will forget about this in no time. It's just

_____ .

(*crisis which looks big, but is only about a small issue*)

**9** I can assure you that this government will not be
_____ by this little piece of scandal.
(*forced to change direction*)

**10** The party became a bit self-satisfied after its
_____ in the general election.
(*very decisive win*)

**11** After that advert which showed a rabbit smoking a cigarette,
there was _____ .
(*a huge number of negative reactions*)

**12** It all seems OK now, but I fear that this is just

_____ .

(*the quiet time which precedes a serious crisis*)

 Check out Tests 32, 39 and 40 for more practice with idioms.

# 43 Cartoons 2

Write the correct letter under each cartoon.

a    Either we've been burgled, or your father lost the remote control.

b    I can't defend you if I know you are guilty. But if you don't tell me where the money is hidden, you can't afford me.

c    Don't feel intimidated, Mr Allsop.

d    That's the Burtons' farm. They're hypochondriacs.

e    They look pretty revolting. But they're very nutritious.

f    Would you remind me, Tracey – am I hiring or firing Mr Willis?

_____c_____

_____

**3**

_____

**4**

_____

**5**

_____

**6**

_____

# 44 Too many words about universities

Replace the words in bold type with a single word from the box.

---

anthropologist   archaeologist   conference   ~~dissertation~~   journal
laboratory   lecture   paper   postgraduate   research   sabbatical
seminar   sociologist   specialism   statistician

---

**1**   As part of our MA course, we have to do a **very long essay with an element of original research** ( _dissertation_ ). The marks we get for this count towards our final result.

---

**2**   Instead of taking notes, I sometimes use a tape to record the **talk given by a member of staff and attended by lots of students** ( _____ ).

---

**3**   Occasionally we have a **discussion with a smaller number of students, chaired by a member of staff** ( _____ ). We have to prepare contributions, and it can be quite stressful.

---

**4**   My economics professor went to a conference in Singapore and presented a **summary of a piece of research** ( _____ ) on free trade and exchange rates.

---

**5**   I'm afraid Doctor Kopala is not available. She is on a **one-year paid break from teaching, in which research is carried out** ( _____ ).

---

**6**   I feel that it's important for me to attend this **big meeting of academics from different places** ( _____ ).

---

**7** I am preparing this paper for publication in a **specialist academic magazine** ( _____ ).

**8** I am a zoologist, but my **particular area of expertise and knowledge** ( _____ ) is temperature control mechanisms in marine mammals. Are you interested in that?

**9** Professor Blumenfeld is a **person who studies the way people operate in society, the dynamics of class and so on** ( _____ ).

**10** In Papua New Guinea I met an **academic who studies humans, concentrating on traditional cultures** ( _____ ).

**11** Egypt is a wonderful place for an **academic who studies history through the physical remains of ancient civilizations** ( _____ ).

**12** This is not just a medical question. We need a **person who understands and interprets confusing mathematical data** ( _____ ).

**13** We now work in a new **building equipped with scientific equipment, set up especially for research and teaching** ( _____ ).

**14** This department offers many **higher** courses, **for those who already have a first degree** ( _____ ).

**15** For a doctorate, you have to do your own original **study and investigation into an aspect of your subject** ( _____ ).

# 45 A breath of fresh air

Complete the sentences using words from the box.

> breath    clap    flash    gust    hint    moment    piece    pinch
> speck    spell    stretch    ~~stroke~~    touch    trace    wink

**1**   She had an amazing __*stroke*__ of luck with her website name
Buy.com – an international company bought it from her for
$1 million.

**2**   Let's go out and get a _____ of fresh air.

**3**   Take everything he says with a _____ of salt. Remember his
story about being a karate black belt? Pure fantasy.

**4**   A rather insignificant _____ of lightning was followed by an
ear-splitting _____ of thunder – it was weird.

**5**   This _____ of road is an accident black-spot, and no action is
being taken to improve it.

**6**   So, the week will start with a _____ of warm weather, but
don't expect it to last.

**7** At the first _____ of trouble, we are out of here – right?

**8** I was so worried about you – I didn't get a _____ of sleep.

**9** It's only a _____ of dust. Just splash your eye with water – and stop complaining.

**10** A sudden _____ of wind pulled the tent out of our hands, and we had to start again.

**11** He took the gold medal, but his _____ of glory was to be short-lived. A drug test proved positive and he was immediately stripped of the honour.

**12** Come on, let me join you in this business deal. I want a _____ of the action.

**13** I feel that the stainless steel chairs add a _____ of class to the place. Don't you agree?

**14** The police have found a _____ of blood on his jacket. They are holding him for questioning.

 The most general word of this type is *a bit*. You can say *a bit of luck, a bit of trouble, a bit of sleep, a bit of road*, a bit of almost anything, in fact!

# 46 Newspaper misprints

Underline and correct the misprints in these newspaper extracts.

**1**
According to a recent survey, 49% of houses in the country are not adequately <u>insulted.</u>

*insulated*

**2**
Customs officers were accepting brides in exchange for co-operation with the drug smugglers.

_____

**3**
Satan wedding dress, white and pink, beautiful, size 14: for sale £250 o.n.o.

_____

**4**
The conference was attended by Greenpeace, Friends of the Earth and other groups interested in conversation.

_____

**5**
The judge said she was giving a severe sentence which would act as a detergent to others tempted by computer fraud.

_____

**6**
Window, youthful 48, seeks professional man for friendship / romance.

_____

**7**
The choir of the Church of the Holy Trinity, Liverpool, sins regularly at festivals around the country.

_____

**8**
The Almahari, an Egyptian restaurant in Knightsbridge, serves exquisite deserts.

_____

**9** The company is finding it increasingly hard to get killed software engineers.

**10** Mr Pertini, now in hospital with a back injury, said, 'I was just moving the lawn – something I've done many times before.'

**11** The party on board the yacht had to be called off, owing to the gale-force winds. Guests of up to 80mph were recorded in the area.

**12** The London restaurant guide has 128 pages of useful information, gathered from various sauces.

**13** Among other exotic pets, Mrs Lavender has a carrot that talks.

**14** Ms Francis, writer of several bestselling novels, lives on the third story of a block of flats in Edinburgh.

**15** The Atomic Energy Authority has been criticized for its management of unclear waste.

Check out Tests 34 and 38 for more practice with error correction.

# 47 Take away two letters

Take away two letters from each of the following words to make a new word.

1   disguised   →   __*disused*__   : abandoned, no longer used

2   executive   →   _____ : to kill legally

3   smooth   →   _____ : black powder left by burning coal

4   deliberate   →   _____ : to make free

5   feeling   →   _____ : to throw roughly

6   excite   →   _____ : the way out

7   install   →   _____ : a shop in an open market

8   marine   →   _____ : the hair on a horse's or lion's neck

9   remember   →   _____ : someone who belongs to the club

10   mineral   →   _____ : someone who digs out coal, gold etc

11   saving   →   _____ : to make music with your voice

12   release   →   _____ : to rent or hire

13   spine   →   _____ : like a needle

14   spite   →   _____ : a big hole in the ground

15   scarce   →   _____ : to be concerned

16   surgeon   →   _____ : to push forward all together

17   sweat   →   _____ : to consume orally

18   stripe   →   _____ : an excursion

19   funnel   →   _____ : petrol, coal and so on

20   triangle   →   _____ : to get all mixed up

21   switch   →   _____ : skin irritation

22   follow   →   _____ : to move smoothly, like a river

# 48 Moods, states and feelings

Complete the sentences using words from the box.

---

confused ~~drowsy~~ faint fragile introspective listless
nostalgic peckish psyched up relieved tense

---

**1** Tiredness can kill. If you start to feel __*drowsy*__ when you're driving, stop as soon as you can.

**2** It's normal to feel a little bit _____ before a performance. But you have to get over it.

**3** Anyone feeling _____ ? I've made a few sandwiches, and there's tea or juice.

**4** Oh, thank goodness you're safe! I'm so _____ . I was imagining all sorts of horrors.

**5** If someone feels _____ , get them to sit down straightaway as there is a danger of them falling. Stay with them, and offer them a drink of water.

**6** She's been _____ for weeks, just moping around the house. Is it a mood, or could it be something medical?

**7** He's been hurt a lot by the break-up. He's a bit _____ at the moment, so treat him with care.

**8** I'm _____ . It's all too ... I don't know. I don't understand what's happening to me.

**9** She's a great coach. She manages to get the team _____ to just the right level before a game.

**10** She's going through an _____ phase, trying to come to terms with herself. Her therapist is very helpful.

**11** Times are hard for many Russians, and some feel _____ about the old soviet system.

# 49 Words beginning with de-

Write the words defined below in the boxes on the right.

1   A formal discussion on a topic by a group of people. (n)

2   Something you do when you play cards. (vb)

3   Lacking in something. (adj)

4   To pull down a building. (vb)

5   Device for unscrambling TV signals. (n)

6   Reliable. (adj)

7   To ask (strongly) for something. (vb)

8   A date or time before which something must be done. (n)

9   Government of the people, by the people, for the people. (n)

10  Washing-up liquid. (n)

11  A type of seat (very popular on British beaches). (n)

12  You put it under your arms to stop the smell of sweat. (n)

13  To win a victory over someone; to beat someone. (vb)

14  Not accidental. (adj)

15  To dislike very much. (vb)

| | | | | | | | | |
|---|---|---|---|---|---|---|---|---|
| **1** | D | E | B | A | T | E | | |
| **2** | D | E | | | | | | |
| **3** | D | E | F | | | | | T |
| **4** | D | E | | | L | | | |
| **5** | D | E | | | | R | | |
| **6** | D | E | | | | D | | L |
| **7** | D | E | | A | | | | |
| **8** | D | E | | | L | | | |
| **9** | D | E | | | | R | | Y |
| **10** | D | E | | E | | | N | |
| **11** | D | E | | | C | | | R |
| **12** | D | E | | | O | | N | |
| **13** | D | E | F | | | | | |
| **14** | D | E | | | | E | | T |
| **15** | D | E | | E | | | | |

A common meaning of *de-* as a prefix is to undo or reverse the action of the verb: **de**regulate, **de**flate, **de**-ice, **de**compress, **de**criminalize, **de**celerate. Can you think of any more examples?

# 50 Right or wrong?

Are the words in bold type in the following sentences used correctly or not?
Explain what's wrong with the ones that are not correct.

|   |   | right | wrong |
|---|---|---|---|
| 1 | A **malevolent** person has a heart of gold. | ☐ | ✓ |
| 2 | He had the job before me. He was my **predecessor**. | ☐ | ☐ |
| 3 | A road with ice on it is called a **slip road**. | ☐ | ☐ |
| 4 | A student who doesn't work hard enough is known as an **understudy**. | ☐ | ☐ |
| 5 | He has a lot of **personnel** and family problems. | ☐ | ☐ |
| 6 | The killer in Psycho stuffs dead birds. He's an amateur **taxidermist**. | ☐ | ☐ |
| 7 | Her parents are very wealthy. Her father's a **marquee**. | ☐ | ☐ |
| 8 | He works for an advertising agency. He's a **copywriter**. | ☐ | ☐ |
| 9 | I had to sack her for incompetence – a very **tasteless** task. | ☐ | ☐ |

|  |  | right | wrong |
|---|---|:---:|:---:|

**10** If something is **fragile** it means it has a sweet or pleasant smell. ☐ ☐

**11** If you're suffering from **amnesia**, you've lost your memory. ☐ ☐

**12** **Inflammable** is the opposite of flammable. ☐ ☐

**13** It's not **comprehensive** – I mean, no – one can understand it. ☐ ☐

**14** She's written fifty-eight novels. She's really **prolific**. ☐ ☐

**15** You'll need to use a lot of **workforce** to lift that lift that piece of concrete. ☐ ☐

Mrs Malaprop in the 18th century play *The Rivals* by Sheridan misused so many words that such mistakes are known as *malapropisms*. For example, she said *illiterate him from your memory* (it should be *obliterate*). And she said *as headstrong as an allegory on the banks of the Nile*. What should that be?

# 51 Who wrote what?

Try to work out who wrote the books below. Choose from the following authors.

Anna Gramm    Dinah Mite    I C Waters    I Malone    I O More
Ivor Pett    Justin Case    Lotta Kidz    Miss T Day    Percy Vere
R U Strong    Robin Banks    Roland Coffey    ~~Sandy Shaw~~    U C Friends

**1**

*Holidays by the Sea*

by ___Sandy Shaw___

**2**

**Get Rich Quick**
**£££££££££££**

by _____

**3**

**MiXeD Up LeTTers**

by _____

**4**

**Never Give Up**

by _____

**5**

*Preparing for the Unexpected*

by _____

**6**

**Demolition with Explosives**

by _____

**7**

**My Marriage Break-up**

by _____

**8**

**How to Manage a Large Family**

by _____

**9**

≡ *Quick* ≡
*Breakfasts*

by _____

_____

**10**

**The Antarctic Ocean**

by _____

_____

**11**

**Test Your Muscles**

by _____

_____

**12**

**Why it's Good to Throw Parties**

by _____

_____

**13**

**Getting a BIGGER Bank Loan**

by _____

_____

**14**

**My Cat**

by _____

_____

**15**

**A Foggy Morning**

by _____

_____

# 52 Homophones

In these pairs (not pears!) of sentences, the missing words sound the same but are spelt differently.

**1**   Breathe in that fresh sea ___air___ .

Prince William is the ___heir___ to the throne.

**2**   She won a silver _____ at the Olympics.

Don't _____ in my affairs.

**3**   A _____ of shoes.

Would you like an apple or a _____ ?

**4**   She wears a lovely fresh _____ by Calvin Klein.

$4.99? Why not add a _____ and make it five dollars?

**5**   We had to _____ the broken-down car to a garage.

I dropped the box on my foot and broke my big _____ .

**6**   How much is the train _____ ?

She got more than me. It's not _____ .

**7**   We can't row the boat. An _____ is missing.

Gold is extracted from _____ .

**8**   Do you come to this _____ often?

Sole and _____ are flat fish.

**9**   To be quite _____ , I don't like it.

It only costs one _____ in Paris.

**10** As American as apple _____ .

The Greek letter _____ is used in maths to calculate area of a circle.

**11** During the _____ of King George III.

Take an umbrella in case of _____ .

**12** A _____ is bigger than a rabbit.

Comb your _____ . It looks awful.

**13** A building _____ is a dangerous place.

We caught _____ of her only briefly.

**14** Please come home. We have _____ you terribly.

It's not really fog – more of a light _____ .

**15** He _____ from side to side, as if drunk.

They're not shiny leather – they're _____ .

 Of course, homophones are one of the features of English that cause spelling problems. People write things like *she past the exam* (what is the mistake here?) Perhaps the biggest source of confusion is a group of three homophones, all of which are common words: *there*, *their* and *they're*.

# 53 One word, two meanings

Read the two definitions for each word and complete the crossword.

## Across

**3** a) general, including everything  b) a coat for dirty work (7)

**4** a) happy, satisfied    b) what a text contains (7)

**5** a) holds up a building    b) section of text in a newspaper (6)

**6** a) massive and sudden political change
b) wheel or part of a machine going round (10)

**10** a) look after, repair e.g. a building    b) assert, say strongly (8)

**13** a) you pass or fail it at school    b) a close check (11)

**15** a) where a dead person is buried    b) very serious (5)

**17** a) container for petrol, water etc
b) military vehicle with big gun (4)

**18** a) an insect that jumps    b) strange but popular English sport (7)

**19** a) part of forehead    b) religious building (Hindu, Roman, etc.) (6)

## Down

**1** a) opposite of the city    b) a state with a flag, government, etc. (7)

**2** a) a booklet with instructions    b) by hand (6)

**3** a) done by a surgeon    b) the way something works (9)

**5** a) being found guilty by a court    b) strong opinion (10)

**7** a) an ordinary soldier    b) not public (7)

**8** a) nice season of the year    b) often found inside a mattress (6)

**9** a) a metal tool    b) a place to store data on the computer (4)

**11** a) to say you were wrong    b) let someone in (5)

**12** a) gases from a car    b) to make tired (7)

**14** a) a newspaper story    b) a thing, an item (7)

**16** a) not very clear    b) to become unconscious (5)

Homophones, like the ones in Test 52, are words with different spellings but the same sound. The pairs of words in this test have the same spelling **and** the same sound; the technical term for such words is *homonyms*. Most homonyms are really just different uses of the same word; for example, the historian's *revolution* and the engineer's *revolution* are obviously related. But some homonyms really have totally separate meanings and origins, like *bear* (the animal) and *bear* (the verb).

# 54 Choose the best word

Choose the best word to complete each sentence.

1    He fell while playing tennis and _grazed_ his knee.

a) sliced   (b) grazed   c) slashed   d) skimmed

2    It is usually difficult to _____ the words of songs.

a) overhear   b) make up   c) identify   d) make out

3    At the wedding reception, the best man _____ the side of his glass lightly with a knife to get the guests' attention.

a) stroked   b) tapped   c) hit   d) beat

4    Excuse me, waiter. Any chance of changing this cup? It's _____ .

a) faulty   b) broken   c) defective   d) chipped

5    You'll have to speak up. My great-grandmother is rather _____ of hearing.

a) hard   b) difficult   c) unsure   d) bad

6    She was so _____ in the book she was reading that she didn't notice me come into the room.

a) impressed   b) mesmerized   c) fascinated   d) engrossed

7    I can't stop now, Marisa. I'm a bit _____ for time. I'll phone you later.

a) lack   b) short   c) pushed   d) rushed

8    _____ will be served during the interval.

a) Refreshments   b) Groceries   c) Nourishment   d) Supplies

**9**   You're off to Sri Lanka? What an extraordinary _____ . So am I.

a) chance  b) fate  c) luck  d) coincidence.

**10**   Two of the actors got the _____ in the middle of the performance. Typical amateurs!

a) laughter  b) chuckles  c) giggles  d) sniggers

**11**   In _____ , women live longer than men in most countries.

a) average  b) the whole  c) general  d) generally

**12**   You may be a good singer, but it is _____ unlikely that you will make it big. Looks are important, too.

a) greatly  b) largely  c) highly  d) almost

**13**   A lot of people try to make use of _____ in the law to pay less tax.

a) loopholes  b) shortages  c) gaps  d) clauses

**14**   Microsoft _____ the software industry.

a) overcomes  b) overwhelms  c) dominates  d) controls

**15**   Police are _____ the crime using DNA fingerprinting.

a) researching  b) investigating  c) checking  d) inspecting

A dictionary may help you when you do this test. But with these subtle differences between words, the dictionary often lets you down; it just doesn't give the example you need. The only way to achieve this kind of proficiency in any language is – you've guessed it! – reading. With extensive reading, you will pick up all these subtleties painlessly – in fact, not just painlessly, but with pleasure!

# 55 Rhyming words

Write the answers to the following questions.

1   Which word means *intelligent* and rhymes with *sight?*   _bright_

2   Which word means *spacious* and rhymes with *gloomy?*   _____

3   Which word means *attic* and rhymes with *soft?*   _____

4   Which word means *avarice* and rhymes with *need?*   _____

5   Which word means *kill* and rhymes with *weigh?*   _____

6   Which word means *begin* and rhymes with *fence?*   _____

7   Which word means *happen* and rhymes with *fir?*   _____

8   Which word means *wander* and rhymes with *home?*   _____

9   Which word means *huge* and rhymes with *pence?*   _____

10  Which word means *accomplish* and rhymes with *sleeve?*   _____

11  Which word means *strong* and rhymes with *stuff?*   _____

12  Which word means *encourage* and rhymes with *merge?*   _____

13  Which word means *be hungry* and rhymes with *carve?*   _____

14  Which word means *something you say to God* and
    rhymes with *fair?*   _____

15  Which word means *undisciplined* and rhymes with
    *forty?*   _____

When you do this test, don't forget that rhymes sound the same but may be
spelt very differently. *Ought* rhymes with *sort* (and *taught, taut, court*), but
*enough* doesn't rhyme with *through*!

# 56 Verbs and nouns

Complete the phrases using words from the box.

achieve    acquit    adjourn    apply for    award    catch    celebrate
compose    confess    demolish    deny    earn    express    extinguish
forge    influence    inherit    invest    investigate    pay

| | | |
|---|---|---|
| **1** | To _____demolish_____ | an old building |
| **2** | To _____ | a fire |
| **3** | To _____ | a crime, a mystery |
| **4** | To _____ | a birthday, a victory |
| **5** | To _____ | a living |
| **6** | To _____ | a decision |
| **7** | To _____ | success |
| **8** | To _____ | a job, a work permit |
| **9** | To _____ | a wish, an opinion |
| **10** | To _____ | attention, someone a compliment |
| **11** | To _____ | a meeting |
| **12** | To _____ | sight of someone |
| **13** | To _____ | your guilt |
| **14** | To _____ | a fortune, a house |
| **15** | To _____ | a prize, a medal |
| **16** | To _____ | music |
| **17** | To _____ | a banknote, a passport |
| **18** | To _____ | an accusation |
| **19** | To _____ | an accused person |
| **20** | To _____ | money, capital |

# 57 Language crossword

Read the clues and complete the crossword.

## Across

**2** Two words with the same meaning. (7)

**6** *Look up, rip off* and *check out* are all _____ verbs. (7)

**8** A sentence with *if* is known as a _____ . (11)

**10** The way your voice goes up and down as you speak. (10)

**12** Formal word for a *question form*. (13)

**13** For example: a, e, o. (5)

**14** For example: *by, through, at*. (11)

**15** For example: *Every cloud has a silver lining*. (7)

## Down

**1** A question which does not expect an answer. (10)

**3** Verbs such as *may, can, must*. (5)

**4** A word like *and, but, while*. (11)

**5** For example: *t, s, b, h, x*. (9)

**6** *Eating* is a present one, *eaten* is a past one. (10)

**7** A word that sounds the same as another word, but is spelt differently and has a completely different meaning. (9)

**9** A word with same letters as another word, but in a different order, e.g. *danger* and *garden*. (7)

**11** For example: *to meet, to kiss, to forget*. (10)

**12** A phrase such as *call it a day*. (5)

# 58 Crazy definitions

Match the words in the box to their rather unusual definitions.

archaeologist  ~~baby~~  bread  classic  illegal  intense  optimist
postman  prune  sense of humour  soap  three-course meal
vacuum cleaner  warehouse  woolly jumper

1  ___baby___ : Something with a noise at one end and a smell at the other.

2  _____ : Something possessed by people who laugh at your jokes.

3  _____ : Something that everybody wants to have read but nobody wants to read.

4  _____ : A broom with a stomach.

5  _____ : A sick bird of prey.

6  _____ : What you say when you are lost.

7  _____ : Where campers sleep.

8  _____ : A plum that has sunbathed too much.

9  _____ : Someone whose career is in ruins.

10  _____ : Shampoo for bald people.

11  _____ : Two chips and a pea.

12  _____ : Raw toast.

13  _____ : Someone who gets the sack as soon as he starts work.

14  _____ : A cross between a sheep and a kangaroo.

15  _____ : Someone who sees a half empty bottle and says it's half full.

Several of these definitions are based on word play or puns. That is the basis of much English-speaking humour. A girl says *I'm going to pick up my prints,* meaning **get my photos from the shop;** her friend says *Which prince is that – Prince William?* But beware: if overused, puns can become very irritating.

# 59 Match the sentences

Match the sentences 1–10 with the responses a–j.

| | | | |
|---|---|---|---|
| 1 | Could you extend the deadline? | a | Don't be ridiculous. I am not a spy. |
| 2 | You should get in touch with your solicitor. | b | Good – so we'll see you on Friday. |
| 3 | I'll have to cancel the meeting. | c | You mean – by taking bribes? |
| 4 | I'm calling to confirm our arrangement. | d | I think we should maintain altitude, with those mountains ahead. |
| 5 | The signal is fading, Captain. | | |
| 6 | He's abusing his position as a police officer. | e | But by how much? Only half a million dollars. |
| 7 | We're losing pressure. We'll have to descend. | f | Don't be pathetic. Why not just postpone it? |
| 8 | We've exceeded our targets again this year. | g | OK. You can have another day. |
| 9 | Why are you frowning? | h | Just try to get their position, OK? |
| 10 | You are betraying your country. | i | I think I should be able to sort this out without resorting to the law. |
| | | j | Oh, money worries, among other things. |

# 60 British and American English

Complete the table of British and American words using words/phrases from the box.

> car park    city centre    ~~deck of cards~~    first floor
> first year undergraduate    garden    liquor store    pacifier    period
> postman    shoestring    term    trainers    vacation

| | AMERICAN ENGLISH | BRITISH ENGLISH |
|---|---|---|
| 1 | *deck of cards* | pack of cards |
| 2 | downtown | |
| 3 | | ground floor |
| 4 | freshman | |
| 5 | | off-licence |
| 6 | mailman | |
| 7 | | lace |
| 8 | sports shoes | |
| 9 | | full stop |
| 10 | yard | |
| 11 | semester | |
| 12 | | dummy |
| 13 | parking lot | |
| 14 | | holiday |

 Will American English take over in Britain? Probably not. Slang catches on quickly; a recent example is *no way* (*No way am I paying for you lot!*) But nobody in Britain is starting to say *sidewalk* instead of *pavement*, or *gas* instead of *petrol*, however many American films they watch.

# Answers

## Test 1

| | |
|---|---|
| badger 4 | newt 5 |
| bat 6 | otter 3 |
| deer 1 | slug 8 |
| eel 12 | sparrow 9 |
| hedgehog 2 | swallow 11 |
| mole 7 | woodpecker 10 |

## Test 2

| | |
|---|---|
| 1 flight | 7 outing |
| 2 travel | 8 package holiday |
| 3 journey | 9 hike |
| 4 voyage | 10 tour |
| 5 cruise | 11 expedition |
| 6 trip | 12 safari |

## Test 3

| | |
|---|---|
| 1 asset | 9 route |
| 2 boredom | 10 stripes |
| 3 signed | 11 range |
| 4 dial | 12 marine |
| 5 hint | 13 verse |
| 6 ideals | 14 several |
| 7 lied | 15 prides |
| 8 braille | |

*garden* is an anagram of *danger*

## Test 4

1 gone off
2 gave ... away
3 goes back
4 getting ... down
5 getting at
6 went out
7 turn ... down
8 drop in
9 came up with
10 get round
11 handed in
12 passed away

## Test 5

| | |
|---|---|
| 1 versatile | 9 tolerant |
| 2 gullible | 10 weird |
| 3 illiterate | 11 tough |
| 4 clumsy | 12 genuine |
| 5 elegant | 13 dynamic |
| 6 intellectual | 14 cynical |
| 7 skilful | 15 intimidating |
| 8 superstitious | |

## Test 6

| | | | | | |
|---|---|---|---|---|---|
| 1 eyelash | 8 thigh | 15 heart |
| 2 eyelid | 9 shin | 16 lung |
| 3 pupil | 10 sole | 17 liver |
| 4 nostril | 11 calf | 18 kidney |
| 5 iris | 12 palm | 19 spine |
| 6 armpit | 13 knuckle | 20 skull |
| 7 vein | 14 artery | 21 ribs |

## Test 7

| | |
|---|---|
| 1 prison | 9 aeroplane |
| 2 newspaper | 10 window |
| 3 bed | 11 funeral |
| 4 car | 12 chess |
| 5 astrology | 13 castle |
| 6 watch | 14 football |
| 7 cat | 15 farm |
| 8 camera | |

## Test 8

| Across | Down |
|---|---|
| 1 temporary | 1 transparent |
| 4 amateur | 2 approximately |
| 6 suspicious | 3 generous |
| 10 unreliable | 5 horizontal |
| 11 voluntary | 7 senior |
| | 8 superior |
| | 9 blunt |

## Test 9

| | |
|---|---|
| 1 food chain | 8 wind turbine |
| 2 pesticide | 9 renewable |
| 3 fertilizer | 10 hydroelectric |
| 4 exhaust | 11 rechargeable |
| 5 biodiversity | 12 residues |
| 6 conservation | 13 consumption |
| 7 genetically | 14 erosion |
| modified (GM) | 15 exploitation |

## Test 10

| | |
|---|---|
| 1 disability | 9 continually |
| 2 basically | 10 disobedience |
| 3 artistic | 11 globalization |
| 4 unreasonable | 12 unhelpful |
| 5 actions | 13 disqualified |
| 6 applicable | 14 precision |
| 7 comparatively | 15 dramatic |
| 8 confidential | |

## Test 11
1 caught a glimpse of
2 distinguish
3 Look
4 watch
5 catch his eye
6 notice
7 glanced
8 recognized
9 peered
10 observing

## Test 12
| | | | |
|---|---|---|---|
| 1 flock | | 9 | board |
| 2 bunch | | 10 | fleet |
| 3 cast | | 11 | pack |
| 4 crowd | | 12 | gang |
| 5 herd | | 13 | bunch |
| 6 swarm | | 14 | collection |
| 7 pack | | 15 | set |
| 8 shoal | | | |

## Test 13
aluminium foil 11
apron 5
carton 12
chopping board 2
cling film 10
colander 7
draining board 6
electric whisk 4
food processor 3
grater 15
kitchen towel 1
rolling pin 13
sieve 14
timer 9
wok 8

## Test 14
| | | | | | |
|---|---|---|---|---|---|
| 1 in | 6 on | 11 in |
| 2 at | 7 on | 12 for |
| 3 In | 8 by | 13 by |
| 4 out of | 9 in | 14 in |
| 5 in | 10 by | 15 in |

## Test 15
| | | | | | |
|---|---|---|---|---|---|
| 1 b | 3 f | 5 d |
| 2 c | 4 e | 6 a |

## Test 16
1 producer
2 Secretary General
3 foreman
4 manager
5 head teacher
6 chef
7 captain
8 curator
9 principal
10 chair
11 vice chancellor
12 chief executive
13 conductor
14 president
15 editor
16 governor
17 admiral
18 director
19 consultant
20 spokesperson

## Test 17
| | | | |
|---|---|---|---|
| 1 unicorn | | 9 | quartet |
| 2 fortnight | | 10 | pentagon |
| 3 duel | | 11 | binary |
| 4 ambidextrous | | 12 | decade |
| 5 binoculars | | 13 | century |
| 6 doubles | | 14 | millennium |
| 7 twins | | 15 | megabyte |
| 8 triplets | | | |

## Test 18
| | | | |
|---|---|---|---|
| 1 altered | | 9 | shade |
| 2 blinked | | 10 | possibly |
| 3 electrical | | 11 | umpire |
| 4 childish | | 12 | policy |
| 5 rumour | | 13 | financial |
| 6 cycle | | 14 | morale |
| 7 disused | | 15 | convenient |
| 8 counsellor | | | |

## Test 19
| | | | |
|---|---|---|---|
| 1 comedy | | 6 | horror |
| 2 soap | | 7 | chat show |
| 3 cartoon | | 8 | sci-fi |
| 4 war film | | 9 | romance |
| 5 wildlife programme | | 10 | documentary |

## Test 20
| | | | |
|---|---|---|---|
| 1 | insisted | 7 | stammered |
| 2 | repeated | 8 | explained |
| 3 | demanded | 9 | pleaded |
| 4 | yelled | 10 | complained |
| 5 | whispered | 11 | lisped |
| 6 | boasted | 12 | sighed |

## Test 21
1 let ... off
2 go through with
3 came round
4 put up with
5 go over
6 got round to
7 fall apart
8 Cut out
9 get out of
10 put ... up
11 putting ... off
12 get through to
13 works out
14 putting ... on
15 go on about

## Test 22
1st Emerald Isle
2nd Dot Com
3rd Miss Piggy

## Test 23
| | | | |
|---|---|---|---|
| 1 | sixth | 11 | betray |
| 2 | decade | 12 | cellar |
| 3 | weary | 13 | bishop |
| 4 | lanky | 14 | breed |
| 5 | recipe | 15 | enclose |
| 6 | dreary | 16 | faith |
| 7 | income | 17 | delight |
| 8 | rugby | 18 | grasp |
| 9 | screen | 19 | mineral |
| 10 | extend | 20 | resign |

## Test 24
| | | | |
|---|---|---|---|
| 1 | defence | 9 | charge |
| 2 | arrest | 10 | juvenile |
| 3 | lawyer | 11 | sentence |
| 4 | evidence | 12 | bail |
| 5 | verdict | 13 | prosecution |
| 6 | prove | 14 | committed |
| 7 | witness | 15 | court |
| 8 | fine | | |

## Test 25
**Across**
1 bar code
4 spreadsheet
5 ISP
7 folder
8 word processing
11 database
12 scanner
13 crash
14 monitor

**Down**
2 cordless
3 fonts
4 spellchecker
6 pirated
7 format
8 paste
10 install

## Test 26
1 autumn, seasons
2 barrel, containers
3 rectangle, shapes
4 because, conjunctions
5 five eighths, fractions
6 botany, sciences
7 etc., abbreviations
8 onyx, gems
9 methane, gases
10 swallow, birds
11 in, prepositions
12 cholera, diseases
13 novelist, writers
14 abstract, paintings
15 spreadsheet, programs

## Test 27
| | | | | | |
|---|---|---|---|---|---|
| 1 | score | 6 | smile | 11 | train |
| 2 | scare | 7 | smell | 12 | grain |
| 3 | scale | 8 | spell | 13 | grape |
| 4 | whale | 9 | spoil | 14 | graze |
| 5 | while | 10 | Spain | 15 | erase |

## Test 28
1 modem – d
2 hypothesis – i
3 harvest – l
4 salmon – n
5 hypnotist – a
6 heel – c
7 collarless – j
8 syringe – k
9 humble – m
10 grater – b
11 trout – g
12 skate – o
13 recipe – f
14 navel – e
15 tune – h

## Test 29

| | | | |
|---|---|---|---|
| 1 | stumbled | 6 | plodded |
| 2 | skipped | 7 | loitered |
| 3 | staggered | 8 | tramped |
| 4 | limped | 9 | crawled |
| 5 | strolled | 10 | leapt |

## Test 30

| | | | |
|---|---|---|---|
| 1 | disturbing | 6 | moving |
| 2 | realistic | 7 | terrifying |
| 3 | gripping | 8 | irritating |
| 4 | fascinating | 9 | exquisite |
| 5 | dull | 10 | striking |

## Test 31

| | | | | | |
|---|---|---|---|---|---|
| 1 | on | 6 | out of | 11 | at |
| 2 | at | 7 | on | 12 | on |
| 3 | in | 8 | into | 13 | for |
| 4 | in | 9 | on | 14 | at |
| 5 | in ... of | 10 | on | 15 | on |

## Test 32

1  out of order
2  call it a day
3  given the sack
4  talking shop
5  out of the blue
6  pull your socks up
7  can't make head or tail of
8  rings a bell
9  make a meal of it
10  went down like a lead balloon
11  has it in for
12  a level playing field

## Test 33

1  takeover
2  profit margins
3  restructure
4  wages
5  salaries
6  forecast
7  subsidiary
8  training
9  economies of scale
10  brand
11  corporate identity
12  market forces
13  output
14  productivity
15  flexible

## Test 34

| | | | |
|---|---|---|---|
| 1 | c | 5 | g |
| 2 | e | 6 | f |
| 3 | a | 7 | d |
| 4 | h | 8 | b |

## Test 35

| | | | |
|---|---|---|---|
| 1 | mane | 9 | fin |
| 2 | saddle | 10 | scales |
| 3 | shoe | 11 | trunk |
| 4 | hoof | 12 | tusk |
| 5 | reins | 13 | beak |
| 6 | whiskers | 14 | feathers |
| 7 | paw | 15 | talons |
| 8 | claws | | |

## Test 36

| | | | | | | | |
|---|---|---|---|---|---|---|---|
| 1 | l | 6 | n | 11 | f | 16 | e |
| 2 | g | 7 | h | 12 | j | 17 | o |
| 3 | r | 8 | m | 13 | b | 18 | t |
| 4 | i | 9 | s | 14 | p | 19 | k |
| 5 | a | 10 | q | 15 | c | 20 | d |

## Test 37

| | | | |
|---|---|---|---|
| 1 | antiseptic | 9 | insomnia |
| 2 | maternity | 10 | prescription |
| 3 | midwife | 11 | diarrhoea |
| 4 | anaesthetic | 12 | infectious |
| 5 | hay fever | 13 | crutches |
| 6 | allergic | 14 | antibodies |
| 7 | transfusion | 15 | dermatologist |
| 8 | sedative | | |

## Test 38

**Pasta**
partisan – parmesan
source – sauce
him – ham

**Meat**
perk – pork
Boer – boar
lame – lamb
stake – steak

**Chicken and Game**
peasant – pheasant
cartridge – partridge

**Fish**
mallet – mullet
place – plaice
tuner – tuna
pawns – prawns

**Vegetables**
beens – beans
parrots – carrots
pleas – peas

**Test 39**

| | | | |
|---|---|---|---|
| 1 | a hatter | 11 | a parrot |
| 2 | a dodo | 12 | a rock |
| 3 | a feather | 13 | a picture |
| 4 | clockwork | 14 | brass |
| 5 | a bat | 15 | a cucumber |
| 6 | life | 16 | toast |
| 7 | ditchwater | 17 | the hills |
| 8 | a fox | 18 | a daisy |
| 9 | nails | 19 | the grave |
| 10 | a bee | 20 | gold |

**Test 40**
1 ruffle feathers
2 empty nest
3 dinosaurs
4 loan shark
5 top dog
6 barking up the wrong tree
7 big fish in a small pond
8 kill the goose that lays the golden eggs
9 more fish in the sea
10 pecking order
11 chicken feed
12 wild horses couldn't tear them apart
13 fly on the wall
14 the cat that got the cream
15 teaching an old dog new tricks

**Test 41**

| | | | | | |
|---|---|---|---|---|---|
| 1 | e | 5 | g | 8 | f |
| 2 | j | 6 | a | 9 | i |
| 3 | h | 7 | b | 10 | c |
| 4 | d | | | | |

**Test 42**
1 see the wood for the trees
2 an uphill struggle
3 froze ... out
4 go with the flow
5 get bogged down
6 find their roots
7 a drop in the ocean
8 a storm in a teacup
9 blown off course

10 landslide victory
11 a huge outcry
12 the calm before the storm

**Test 43**

| | | | | | |
|---|---|---|---|---|---|
| 1 | c | 3 | b | 5 | f |
| 2 | d | 4 | e | 6 | a |

**Test 44**

| | | | |
|---|---|---|---|
| 1 | dissertation | 9 | sociologist |
| 2 | lecture | 10 | anthropologist |
| 3 | seminar | 11 | archaeologist |
| 4 | paper | 12 | statistician |
| 5 | sabbatical | 13 | laboratory |
| 6 | conference | 14 | postgraduate |
| 7 | journal | 15 | research |
| 8 | specialism | | |

**Test 45**

| | | | |
|---|---|---|---|
| 1 | stroke | 8 | wink |
| 2 | breath | 9 | speck |
| 3 | pinch | 10 | gust |
| 4 | flash, clap | 11 | moment |
| 5 | stretch | 12 | piece |
| 6 | spell | 13 | touch |
| 7 | hint | 14 | trace |

**Test 46**
1 insulted – insulated
2 brides – bribes
3 Satan – Satin
4 conversation – conservation
5 detergent – deterrent
6 Window – Widow
7 sins – sings
8 deserts – desserts
9 killed – skilled
10 moving – mowing
11 Guests – Gusts
12 sauces – sources
13 carrot – parrot
14 story – storey
15 unclear – nuclear

**Test 47**

| | | | |
|---|---|---|---|
| 1 | disused | 10 | miner |
| 2 | execute | 11 | sing |
| 3 | soot | 12 | lease |
| 4 | liberate | 13 | pin |
| 5 | fling | 14 | pit |
| 6 | exit | 15 | care |
| 7 | stall | 16 | surge |
| 8 | mane | 17 | eat |
| 9 | member | 18 | trip |

| | |
|---|---|
| 19 fuel | 21 itch |
| 20 tangle | 22 flow |

**Test 48**

| | |
|---|---|
| 1 drowsy | 7 fragile |
| 2 tense | 8 confused |
| 3 peckish | 9 psyched up |
| 4 relieved | 10 introspective |
| 5 faint | 11 nostalgic |
| 6 listless | |

**Test 49**

| | |
|---|---|
| 1 debate | 9 democracy |
| 2 deal | 10 detergent |
| 3 deficient | 11 deckchair |
| 4 demolish | 12 deodorant |
| 5 decoder | 13 defeat |
| 6 dependable | 14 deliberate |
| 7 demand | 15 detest |
| 8 deadline | |

**Test 50**

1 Wrong. A **malevolent** person wants to harm other people.

2 Right. A **predecessor** is someone who had your job before you.

3 Wrong. A **slip road** is a road for driving off or onto a motorway.

4 Wrong. An **understudy** is an actor who learns a part in a play in case he / she has to replace another actor.

5 Wrong. **Personnel** are people who work in a company or organisation. You have **personal** problems.

6 Right. A **taxidermist** stuffs dead animals.

7 Wrong. A **marquee** is a very large tent. A **marquis** is a member of the nobility.

8 Right. A **copywriter** is someone who writes the words for advertisements.

9 Wrong. **Tasteless** describes food that doesn't have much taste, or a comment or joke that isn't appropriate in a certain situation. A very unpleasant task is **distasteful**.

10 Wrong. If something is **fragile**, it means it is delicate and could easily break. **Fragrant** describes a pleasant smell.

11 Right. **Amnesia** means the loss of memory.

12 Wrong. **Flammable** and **inflammable** have the same meaning.

13 Wrong. **Comprehensive** describes something that includes all the necessary facts and details. **Comprehensible** describes something that is clear or easy to understand.

14 Right. **Prolific** describes an artist or writer who produces many works of art, novels, etc.

15 Wrong. **Workforce** means the people who work in a company or industry.

*allegory* should have been *alligator*

**Test 51**

| | |
|---|---|
| 1 Sandy Shaw | 9 Roland Coffey |
| 2 Robin Banks | 10 I C Waters |
| 3 Anna Gramm | 11 R U Strong |
| 4 Percy Vere | 12 U C Friends |
| 5 Justin Case | 13 I O More |
| 6 Dinah Mite | 14 Ivor Pett |
| 7 I Malone | 15 Miss T Day |
| 8 Lotta Kidz | |

**Test 52**

| | |
|---|---|
| 1 air, heir | 9 frank, franc |
| 2 medal, meddle | 10 pie, pi |
| 3 pair, pear | 11 reign, rain |
| 4 scent, cent | 12 hare, hair |
| 5 tow, toe | 13 site, sight |
| 6 fare, fair | 14 missed, mist |
| 7 oar, ore | 15 swayed, suede |
| 8 place, plaice | |

## Test 53

| Across | | Down | |
|---|---|---|---|
| 3 | overall | 1 | country |
| 4 | content | 2 | manual |
| 5 | column | 3 | operation |
| 6 | revolution | 5 | conviction |
| 10 | maintain | 7 | private |
| 13 | examination | 8 | spring |
| 15 | grave | 9 | file |
| 17 | tank | 11 | admit |
| 18 | cricket | 12 | exhaust |
| 19 | temple | 14 | article |
| | | 16 | faint |

## Test 54

| | | | |
|---|---|---|---|
| 1 | b grazed | 9 | d coincidence |
| 2 | d make out | 10 | c giggles |
| 3 | b tapped | 11 | c general |
| 4 | d chipped | 12 | c highly |
| 5 | a hard | 13 | a loopholes |
| 6 | d engrossed | 14 | c dominates |
| 7 | c pushed | 15 | b investigating |
| 8 | a Refreshments | | |

## Test 55

| | | | |
|---|---|---|---|
| 1 | bright | 9 | immense |
| 2 | roomy | 10 | achieve |
| 3 | loft | 11 | tough |
| 4 | greed | 12 | urge |
| 5 | slay | 13 | starve |
| 6 | commence | 14 | prayer |
| 7 | occur | 15 | naughty |
| 8 | roam | | |

## Test 56

| | | | |
|---|---|---|---|
| 1 | demolish | 11 | adjourn |
| 2 | extinguish | 12 | catch |
| 3 | investigate | 13 | confess |
| 4 | celebrate | 14 | inherit |
| 5 | earn | 15 | award |
| 6 | influence | 16 | compose |
| 7 | achieve | 17 | forge |
| 8 | apply for | 18 | deny |
| 9 | express | 19 | acquit |
| 10 | pay | 20 | invest |

## Test 57

| Across | | Down | |
|---|---|---|---|
| 2 | synonyms | 1 | rhetorical |
| 6 | phrasal | 3 | modal |
| 8 | conditional | 4 | conjunction |
| 10 | intonation | 5 | consonant |
| 12 | interrogative | 6 | participle |
| 13 | vowel | 7 | homophone |
| 14 | preposition | 9 | anagram |
| 15 | proverb | 11 | infinitive |
| | | 12 | idiom |

## Test 58

| | |
|---|---|
| 1 | baby |
| 2 | sense of humour |
| 3 | classic |
| 4 | vacuum cleaner |
| 5 | illegal (ill eagle) |
| 6 | warehouse (where house?) |
| 7 | intense (in tents) |
| 8 | prune |
| 9 | archaeologist |
| 10 | soap |
| 11 | three-course meal |
| 12 | bread |
| 13 | postman |
| 14 | woolly jumper |
| 15 | optimist |

## Test 59

| | | | | | |
|---|---|---|---|---|---|
| 1 | g | 5 | h | 8 | e |
| 2 | i | 6 | c | 9 | j |
| 3 | f | 7 | d | 10 | a |
| 4 | b | | | | |

## Test 60

| | | | |
|---|---|---|---|
| 1 | deck of cards | 8 | trainers |
| 2 | city centre | 9 | period |
| 3 | first floor | 10 | garden |
| 4 | first year | 11 | term |
| | undergraduate | 12 | pacifier |
| 5 | liquor store | 13 | car park |
| 6 | postman | 14 | vacation |
| 7 | shoestring | | |

# Word list

### A
abbreviation 26
absorbed 34
abstract 26
abuse 59
accomplish 55
achieve 56
acquit 56
action 9
adjourn 56
admiral 16
admit 53
aeroplane 7
aggressive 54
air 52
allergic 37
almost 54
alter 18
aluminium foil 13
amateur 8
ambidextrous 17
amnesia 50
anaesthetic 37
anthropologist 44
antibodies 37
antiseptic 37
applicable 10
apply for 56
approximately 8
apron 13
archaeologist 44, 58
arm 36
armpit 6
arrangement 59
arrest 24
artery 6
article 53
artistic 10
asset 3
astrology 7
attic 55
autobiography 28
autumn 26
avarice 55
average 54
award 56

### B
baby 58
bad 54
badger 1
baggage reclaim 41
bail 24
bank loan 51
bar code 25
bark 40
barrel 26, 36
basically 10
bass 28
bat 1, 39
beak 35, 36
bean 38
beat 54
bed 7
bee 39
beef 38
begin 55
betray 23, 59
binary 17
binoculars 17
biodiversity 9
bird 26, 36
bishop 23
blade 36
blink 18
blunt 8
boar 38
board 12
boast 20
Boer 38
book 36, 41
boost 34
boot 28
boredom 3
botany 26
bottle 36
braille 3
branch 36
brand 33
brass 39
bread 23, 58
breadcrumbs 38
breath 45
bribe 46

bride 46
bridegroom 28
broccoli 38
budget 34
bumper 28
bunch 12
butler 28

### C
cabbage 38
calf 6
calm 34
camera 7, 36
cancel 59
captain 16
car 7
car park 60
carburettor 36
care 47
carrot 38, 46
carton 13
cartoon 19
cartridge 38
carve 55
cast 12
castle 7
cat 7
catch 56
celebrate 51, 56
cell 23
cellar 23
cent 52
century 17
chair 16, 36
chance 54
chancellor 34
charge 24
chat show 19
check 54
check in 41
check-out 36
cheese 38
chef 16, 38
chess 7
chess set 36
chicken 38
chicken feed 40

chief constable 16, 34
childish 18
cholera 26
chop 38
chopping board 13
chord 28
chuckle 54
circle 18
city centre 60
clap 45
classic 58
clause 54
claw 35
cling film 13
clockwork 39
close 23
clumsy 5
coincidence 54
colander 13
collarless 28
collection 12
column 53
come 23
come round 21
come up with 4
comedy 19
commit 24
comparatively 10
complain 20
complaint 41
compose 56
comprehensive 50
computer 36
conductor 16
conference 44
confess 56
confidential 10
confirm 59
confused 48
conjunction 26
conservation 9, 46
consultant 16
consumption 9
container 26
content 53
continually 10
control 54
convenient 18
conversation 46
conviction 53
copier 28

copywriter 50
cordless 25, 28
corner 28
corporate identity 33
counsellor 18
country 53
court 24
crash 25
cream 40
creep 29
cricket 53
crowd 12
cruise 2
crutch 37
cucumber 39
curator 16
cut out 21
cutlet 38
cycle 18
cynical 5

**D**
daisy 39
database 25
dead 23
deadline 49, 59
deal 49
dear 23
debate 49
decade 17, 23
deck of cards 60
deckchair 49
declare 41
decoder 49
deer 1
defeat 49
defence 24
deficient 49
deliberate 47, 49
delight 23
demand 20, 49
democracy 49
demolish 49, 56
demolition 51
deny 56
deodorant 49
dependable 49
deposit 28
dermatologist 37
descend 59
desert 46
dessert 46

detergent 46, 49
deterrent 46
detest 49
dial 3
diarrhoea 37
difficult 54
dinosaur 40
director 16
disability 10
disease 26
disguised 47
disobedience 10
disqualify 10
dissertation 44
distinguish 11
disturbing 30
disused 18, 47
ditchwater 39
documentary 19
dodo 39
dominate 54
doubles 17
draining board 13
dramatic 10
dreary 23
drop in 4
drowsy 48
duel 17
dull 30
dynamic 5

**E**
earn 56
eat 47
economies of scale 33
editor 16
eel 1
election 34
electric whisk 13
electrical 18
elegant 5
enclose 23
encourage 34
engrossed 54
erase 27
erosion 9
etc. 26
evidence 24
examination 53
exceed 59
exchange rate 41

excite 47
execute 47
executive 47
exhaust 9, 53
exit 47
expedition 2
explain 20
exploitation 9
explosives 51
express 56
exquisite 30
extend 23, 47, 59
extinguish 56
eye 36
eyelash 6
eyelid 6

**F**
fade 59
faint 48, 53
fair 52, 55
faith 23
fall apart 21
fare 52
farm 7
fascinated 54
fascinating 30
fate 54
feather 35, 39
feeling 47
fence 55
fertilizer 9
file 28, 53
film crew 16
fin 35
financial 18
fine 24
fir 55
first floor 60
fit 23
five-eighths 26
flammable 50
flash 45
fleet 12
flexible 33
flight 2
fling 47
flock 12
flow 47
flower 36
foggy 51

follow 47
font 25
food chain 9
food processor 13
football 7
forecast 33
foreman 16
forge 56
format 25
fortnight 17
fox 39
fraction 26
fragile 48, 50
frame 36
franc 52
frank 52
frown 59
fuel 34, 47
funeral 7
funnel 47

**G**
game 38
gang 12
gap 23, 54
garden 60
garlic 38
gas 26
gear 28
gem 26
general 54
generally 54
generous 8
genetically modified
   (GM) 9
genuine 5
get at 4
get ... down 4
get in touch 59
get out of 21
get round 4
get round to 21
get through to 21
giggle 54
ginger 38
give ... away 4
give up 51
glance 11
glimpse 11
globalization 10
gloomy 55
go back 4

go off 4
go on about 21
go out 4
go over 21
go through with 21
God 55
gold 39
goose 40
govenor 16
grain 27
grant 27, 34
grasp 23
grater 13, 28
grave 39, 53
graze 27, 54
greatly 54
grilled 38
gripping 30
grocer 28
groceries 54
guests 46
gullible 5
gust 45, 46

**H**
hair 52
ham 38
hand in 4
handcuffs 28
handset 28
happen 55
hard 54
hard disk 36
hare 52
harvest 28
hatter 39
hay fever 37
head teacher 16
heart 6
hedgehog 1
heel 28
heir 52
hepatitis 28
herb 38
herd 12
highly 54
hike 2
hill 39
hint 3, 45
historian 28
hit 54
holiday 51

option 28
orange 36
ore 52
organic 38
otter 1
outing 2
output 28, 33
overall 53
overcome 54
overhear 54
overwhelm 54

**P**

pacifier 60
pack 12
package 2
package holiday 3, 41
painting 26
pair 52
palm 6
paper 44
parmesan 38
parrot 38, 39, 46
partisan 38
partridge 38
pass 28
pass away 4
paste 25
pawn 36, 38
paws 35
pay 56
pea 38
pear 52
peasant 38
pecking order 40
peckish 48
peer 11
pence 55
pentagon 17
period 60
perk 38
pesticide 9
petal 36
petrol 34
petrol engine 36
pheasant 38
philosopher 28
photographer 28
physicist 28
pi 52
piano 36

picture 39
pie 52
piece 45
pin 47
pinch 45
pip 36
pirate 25
pit 47
place 38, 52
plaice 38, 52
plea 38
plead 20
plod 29
poem 28
police officer 59
policy 18
poll 34
pond 40
pork 38
position 59
postgraduate 44
postman 58 ,60
prawn 38
precision 10
predecessor 50
prepare 51
preposition 26
prescription 37
president 16
pressure 59
prices 34
pride 3
principal 16
prison 7
private 53
producer 16
productivity 33
profit margins 33
program 26
prolific 50
proposal 34
prosecution 24
protests 34
prove 24
prune 58
psoriasis 28
psyched up 48
pupil 6
push 54
put ... off 21
put ... on 21

put up with 21

**Q**

quartet 17

**R**

rain 52
range 3
ravioli 38
realistic 30
reception 28
rechargeable 9
recipe 23, 28
reckon 41
recognize 11
rectangle 26
red 23
reduce 34
refreshments 54
refugee 34
register 41
reign 52
reins 35
release 47
relieved 48
remember 47
renewable 9
repeat 20
research 44, 54
residues 9
resign 23, 34
restructure 33
revolution 53
rib 6, 28
rifle 36
ripe 23
roast 38
rock 39
rolling pin 13
romance 19
route 3
ruffle feathers 40
rug 23
rugby 23
rumour 18
rush 54

**S**

sabbatical 44
saddle 35
safari 2
sailing boat 36

salary 33
salmon 28
saloon 34
Satan 46
satin 46
sauce 38, 46
sausages 38
saving 47
scale 27, 35
scanner 25
scarce 47
scare 27
scent 52
science 26
sci-fi 19
score 27, 28
screen 23
Secretary General 16
sedative 37
self-catering 41
seminar 44
senior 8
sense of humour 58
sentence 24
set 12
several 3
shade 18
shape 26
shin 6
shoal 12
shoe 35, 36
shoestring 60
shop 23
short 54
shortage 54
shutter 28
sieve 13
sigh 20
sight 52, 55
sign 3, 23
signal 59
sin 46
sing 46, 47
sit 23
site 52
sixth 23
skate 28
sketch 45
skilful 5
skilled 46
skim 55
skip 29

skull 6
slash 54
slice 54
slip road 50
slug 1
smell 27
smile 27
snigger 54
soap 19, 58
soccer 34
sociologist 44
soft 55
sole 6, 36
solicitor 59
soot 47
source 38, 46
spacious 55
spaghetti 38
sparrow 1
specialism 44
speck 45
spell 27, 45
spellchecker 25
spending 34
spinach 38
spine 6, 36, 47
spite 47
spoil 27
spokesperson 16
spokeswoman 34
sporty 55
sprain 27
spreadsheet 25, 26
spring 53
stagger 29
stake 38
stale 23
stall 47
stammer 20
stationery 28
statistician 44
steak 38
steal 34
stew 38
stir-fried 38
storey 46
story 46
striking 30
stripe 47
stripes 3
stroke 45, 54
stroll 29

stuff 55
stumble 29
subsidiary 33
suede 52
superior 8
supermarket 36
superstitious 5
supplies 54
support 34
surge 47
surgeon 47
surveillance system 36
suspicious 8
swallow 1, 26
swarm 12
swayed 52
sweat 47
switch 47
syringe 28

**T**
takeover 33
talon 35
tangle 47
tank 53
tap 54
target 59
tasteless 50
taxidermist 50
teeth 58
temple 53
temporary 8
tend 23
tense 48
term 60
terrifying 30
terrifying 30
thigh 6
three-course meal 58
throat 28
throw parties 51
tide 34
timer 13
toast 39
toe 52
tolerant 5
tomato 38
top dog 40
touch 45
tough 5
tour 2
tow 52

trace 45
train 27
trainee 34
trainers 60
training 33
tramp 29
transfusion 37
transparent 8
travel 2
tray 23
triangle 47
trick 40
trip 2, 47
triplets 17
tripod 28
trout 28
truncheon 28
trunk 35
tuna 38
tune 28
tuner 38
turn … down 4
tusk 35
twig 36
twins 17

**U**
umpire 18
unclear 46
undergraduate 60

understudy 50
undisciplined 55
unexpected 51
unhelpful 10
unicorn 17
unreasonable 10
unreliable 8
unsure 54

**V**
vacation 60
vacuum cleaner 58
veal 38
vein 6
venison 38
verdict 24
versatile 5
verse 3
vice chancellor 16
video camera 36
viewfinder 36
villa 41
voluntary 8
voyage 2

**W**
wages 33
wander 55
war film 19

warehouse 58
watch 7, 11
way 23
weary 23
wedding 51
weigh 55
weird 5
whale 27
while 27
whisker 35
whisper 20
widow 46
wildlife programme 19
wind turbine 9
window 7, 36, 46
wink 45
witness 24
wok 13
woodpecker 1
woolly jumper 58
word processing 25
workforce 50
works out 21
writer 26

**Y**
yelled 20